The Coiner's Wife

Further titles by Maurice Claypole

Drama and fiction

Narrowboat Blues

The Legend of Sidora

A Parting Shot

Textbooks

Controversies in ELT

Artificial Intelligence in Autonomous Language Learning

The Fractal Approach to Teaching English as Foreign Language

The Coiner's Wife

A play in five acts

by Maurice Claypole

LinguaBooks

Maurice Claypole has asserted his right under the Copyright, Designs and Patents Act, 1988 to be identified as the author of this work.

ISBN (paperback edition): 978-1911369622
eISBN (digital edition): 978-1911369806

First edition

Editor: Ann Claypole

A CIP catalogue record for this book is available from the British Library.

Image credits:
Cover figure © Photowitch | Dreamstime.com
Cover landscape © Philip Openshaw | Dreamstime.com

LinguaBooks
Elsie Whiteley Innovation Centre
Hopwood Lane
Halifax HX1 5ER

www.linguabooks.com

Performance Rights

No performances of this work are permitted except with the author's express permission.

A licence issued to perform this play does not include permission to use any incidental music specified in the present work. Licensees are solely responsible for obtaining written permission from the respective copyright owners to use copyrighted music and/or lyrics during the performance of this work. Accordingly, licensees are solely responsible and liable for all music clearances and shall indemnify the copyright owners of this work and their publishers and agents against any costs, expenses, losses and liabilities arising from the use of copyrighted music and/or lyrics by licensees.

Billing and credit requirements

All advertising and publicity material (leaflets, programmes, flyers, posters, etc., including any announcement made via digital or social media) relating to any actual or indented production of this work must include the following billing details, each item of which shall be displayed in a prominent form and position:

[Title of Play]
by [Author]
in association with LinguaBooks

The untold story of Grace Hartley of Cragg Vale, wife of the infamous 18th century counterfeiter, 'King' David Hartley

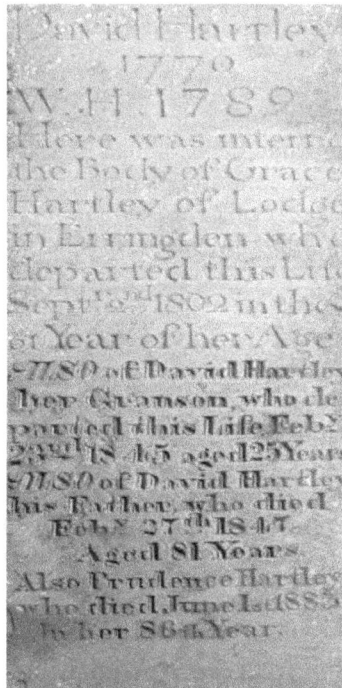

*Grave of David and Grace Hartley
in Heptonstall, West Yorkshire*

The inscription reads:

David Hartley / 1770 / W.H. 1789 / Here was interr'd / the Body of Grace / Hartley of Lodge / in Erringden who / departed this Life / Sepr 2nd 1802 in the / 61 Year of her Age / ALSO of David / her Granson, who de= / parted this Life Feb^y / 23rd 1845 aged 25 Years / ALSO of David / his Father, who died / Feby 27th 1847. / Aged 81 Years. / Also Prudence Hartley / who died June 1st 1883 / in her 86th Year

About the play

At the time of publication, this play is under consideration by the Royal Shakespeare Company as part of the RSC's 37 Plays project but is available for performance elsewhere. Further details on request.

SYNOPSIS

From a remote weaver's cottage in the bleak Yorkshire moors, a gang of counterfeiters (the 'Cragg Vale Coiners') launch a nefarious scheme that threatens to unsettle the currency of 18th century England.

Bound in marriage to their leader, known locally as 'King' David, Grace Hartley is torn between the forces of love, duty and conscience, whilst at the same time struggling with motherhood and the need to keep hunger at bay.

After the counterfeiters' initial success, opposing forces gather, led by William Dighton, Supervisor of Excises, who sets in motion a series of events that have momentous consequences.

This play is based on a true story that has gripped the inhabitants of the Upper Calder Valley for centuries, but has so far received little prominence elsewhere.

The Calder Valley is known to many as the setting for the hit television series *Happy Valley*.

BACKGROUND

The historical characters have previously been the subject of a novel, *The Gallow's Pole* by Benjamin Myers, but this play is not an adaptation of that novel or of any other previous work.

In the interests of authenticity, the historical context and political background have been independently researched, and the story depicted reflects actual events, but characterisations and motivations are the author's own creation. For dramatic purposes, some minor historical details have been changed.

At the time of writing, it is reported that a BBC television adaptation of The Gallow's Pole is in preparation. This can be expected to greatly enhance the popularity and appeal of the subject matter.

A FEMALE VOICE

This play presents the historic and tumultuous events of this episode in history from a woman's point of view. Very little is known about the real Grace Hartley or the other women in this story. In the male-dominated world of the late eighteenth century, documentation focuses almost exclusively on the role played by men. Part of the purpose of this play is to redress this imbalance.

MODERN RELEVANCE

Although the play is set in the past, the themes of poverty, oppression, guilt and revenge are universal in nature and highly applicable to the world of today. Similarly, striking parallels may be drawn between the politics and society of eighteenth-century England and the present day.

TAGLINES

A gripping story of love, betrayal and survival.

Based on true events.

ALTERNATIVE TITLE

Valley of Gold

Table of Contents

Casting and characters

Casting

10 M, 6 F

Characters

(Age in 1766)*

David Hartley (36)	Leader of a gang of coiners
Isaac Hartley (29)	David's brother
William Hartley (63)	Widowed father of David and Isaac
Grace Hartley (25)	Married to David
Bessy Hartley (38)	Married to Isaac
Edie (teenager)	Helper in the Hartley household
Thomas Clayton (36)	Coiner and conspirator
James Broadbent (30)	Coiner and informer
Mathew Normington (27)	Hired killer
Robert Thomas (27)	Hired killer
William Dighton (49)	Excise supervisor and tax collector
Ella Dighton (48)	Married to William Dighton
Mary	Servant to the Dightons
Robert Parker (34)	Solicitor
Ann Parker (50)	Married to Robert Parker
Rockingham (36)	Charles Watson-Wentworth, Marquess of Rockingham, former Prime Minister and now Lord Lieutenant of Yorkshire

In terms of the male characters, there is ample opportunity for doubling.

Minor and ensemble roles:

Coiners, citizens, bailiffs, townsfolk, villagers, servants, messenger, etc. Also Walker, a farmer (in Epilogue only).

If child actors are available, they may appear in domestic scenes, even if not specifically indicated in the script.

For convenience, the Hartleys and other principal characters are referred to by their first names, others by their surnames or role.

* Historical ages are given as a guideline, but most characters can be played by actors of any age. Life expectancy in the 18th century was considerably shorter than today, and the working population also aged faster. William, for example, is considered old at 63.

In comparative terms, David is eleven years older than Grace, and Ann Parker is considerably older than her husband, Robert.

Setting

The action takes place in Yorkshire in the late eighteenth century.

Note on set design

Most of the action takes place in Bell House, a farmer-weaver's cottage on Erringden Moor in Yorkshire and home of the Hartley family. The interior of Bell House features a spinning wheel, a loom, table and chairs and a fireplace. Upstage a door to the back yard, stage left front door and window, stage right door or staircase to sleeping quarters.

Other scenes take place in a variety of inns and taverns, which could all be the same set with minor variations. Street and gaol scenes can be played in front of tabs or using a partial set.

Although a full set is envisaged, the director is free to opt for a minimalist production, suggesting locations by means of furniture and lighting.

Interval

From a point of view of timing, a suitable place for an interval would be between Acts II and III.

The Coiner's Wife

The untold story of Grace Hartley of Cragg Vale,
wife of the infamous 18th century counterfeiter,
'King' David Hartley

The main events take place in the years 1766 – 1770.

The Prologue and Epilogue are set in 1774.

PROLOGUE
(1774)

Bell House. Autumn.

GRACE is packing her belongings. She pauses and addresses the audience.

GRACE

Bell House, my home during those turbulent years when we ruled the world. They have already started to tell wild tales of my dearest David. They say he was touched by the magic spirits of the Valley; they say his mind was taken over by the devil himself; they even say he was hanged in chains on Beacon Hill. But that's all lies. None of that ever occurred in the world of harsh reality. Other things took place, though, momentous events that cost men their lives and ruined their wives and families. From here, stones were thrown into the unforgiving waters of the River Calder, causing ripples that became waves and billowed out to shoot a tremor through the earth, an undulating force that spread from the West Riding of Yorkshire to the moral wilderness of Westminster, making King George quake in his palace and sending his minions scurrying up here to level down the land they call the North, which had dared to test their power.

I don't care what they say; my husband was a good man; he looked after his own, and that's what you've got to do. We'd all have starved otherwise. Next to nowt folks got for the weaving; morning till night at the loom and not a scrap left to show for it at the end. But David changed all that; made us proud, he did. And they followed him; revered him, they did. King David, they called him; now that tells you what sort of man he was. My David, King David. Me? No, I was never a queen; I know my place. When we first came to Bell House from the land of iron and steel, it was a different world; hard winter days of frozen ground and barren earth. Then came the summer blossom; we had the world at our feet, ruled over moor and valley as far as you could walk in a day and beyond.

People will always tell tales, and some of the tales they tell may be true, but so much is just fancy, and in a world where most mortals are formed of base metal, my David was the gold of which legends are born.

So much to tell… But when did it all start? I suppose you could say it started the day we arrived here at Bell House.

ACT I

(1766)

SCENE 1

Bell House. February, 1766.

BESSY is at the spinning wheel. WILLIAM is at the loom.

WILLIAM

They want this shalloon finished by the end of the week. It'll never be done in time. My eyes aren't what they were, let alone my fingers. Even when Rosie was alive, we could hardly keep up.

BESSY

Well, I'm doing my best, William.

WILLIAM

I know, Bessy. You're a dear lass, and I thank the Lord every day that I've got a daughter-in-law like you. I'm so grateful for you and our Isaac mucking in and helping out here. I'd be all on my own otherwise. At least until that eldest son of mine gets back. For what he's worth. It's five years, he's been away. Left me and Rosie to fend for ourselves, he did. And now she's gone, too.

BESSY

Don't be so harsh on him, now. David had to go and learn a trade. Nothing here but the weaving and the farming, and no future in either. And now that he's got new skills, it'll be good for all of us. There's always work for a blacksmith or an iron worker.

16

WILLIAM

Aye well. Let's hope he can get some work here and put some food on the table. I can hardly use a loom nowadays and you and Isaac can't keep on breaking your backs for next to nowt. You've got your own home to look after and your own lives to lead.

BESSY

Well, you've read his letter. He'll be back soon and then maybe you can stop moaning. And I'm so glad it worked out with Grace. Fancy going off to the Midlands to get married!

WILLIAM

Well, it was always the idea that they would come here and help out on the farm as soon as David could get away. And soon there'll be three of them, so I guess there'll be a few changes around here.

BESSY

Well, there you go; cheer up, you old misery. You've got a new grandchild to look forward to.

ISAAC enters from the yard. Farmyard noises (pig, chickens) can be heard when the door is open. He places a basket containing a sparse amount of farm produce (turnips, eggs) on the floor.

ISAAC

(To WILLIAM)

That's the chickens done, and I've fixed the roof on that shed, Dad; you don't have to worry about that any more.

(To BESSY)

Any chance of something hot, love?

BESSY

The pot's on the stove. I'll see to it in a minute.

ISAAC

Right. Well, I just have to go and check on that ewe. She'll be lambing soon. Won't be long.

Exit ISAAC to farmyard.

BESSY leaves the spinning and attends to the stove, starts preparing food.

A dog barks.

BESSY looks out of the window.

BESSY

There's someone coming.

DAVID enters through the front door.

WILLIAM

Well, what a surprise!

DAVID

You knew we'd be coming. It was all agreed.

WILLIAM

Aye, lad, but we didn't know when.

DAVID

And I wrote.

WILLIAM

Yes, got your letter. Something to look forward to, I gather. And I'm looking forward to you making yourself useful around here, an' all.

BESSY

Never mind him, David. Come here, let me look at you.

She holds out her arms in welcome.

Welcome home!

She gives him a brief hug.

WILLIAM stands, appraises DAVID.

WILLIAM

Aye, well, welcome back, lad. You're older, I see. Wiser, too, I hope.

BESSY

Don't be so miserable, William. Say something nice for a change.

WILLIAM

(To David)

Done all right for yourself have you?

DAVID

Can't complain. We've had our ups and downs, but we've done all right.

BESSY

I can tell. Such fine clothes.

WILLIAM

Don't give the lad a big head. He was bad enough when he left home.

BESSY

(Looking round)

Where's Grace?

DAVID

It's been a long haul, and we had to walk part of the way. Cart got stuck in the mud. She's just having a bit of a sit-down. Said I should go on ahead.

BESSY

You must be famished. Let me get you something to eat.

GRACE enters through the front door. She is visibly pregnant and holding a bunch of violets.

GRACE

I picked these. I thought it would be nice to bring something.

BESSY

Oooh, how sweet of you. Violets!

GRACE

They're my favourite flower, so I thought you would like them, too.

BESSY

They're lovely.

GRACE

There were violets everywhere in the garden when I was growing up. My mum loved them. There's something special and uplifting about them. They say the scent alone can bring joy or cure a broken heart.

BESSY arranges the flowers in a vase, places them prominently on the kitchen table.

BESSY

So good to see you, Grace. So glad to have you back. Back where you belong.

WILLIAM

Aye, welcome lass. Good to see you. Must have been awful in the big city. All that dirt and noise.

GRACE

You get used to it. I think you can get used to anything with time. But you're right: it's good to be back. The air's different here.

BESSY

(Indicating GRACE's bump)

When's it due?

GRACE

It'll be a while yet. A couple of months.

BESSY

Well, we'll make sure you're properly looked after here, won't we, William?

WILLIAM

Oh, aye.

ISAAC enters from the yard. Looks around. Takes in the scene.

ISAAC

Hey up, our David. Welcome back. You've put on weight.

DAVID

All muscle, Ha! Ha!

ISAAC

(Indicating DAVID's stomach)

Good, strong eating muscles, then!

Laughter all round.

21

DAVID

You remember Grace?

ISAAC

Of course. Hello, Grace.

GRACE

Beat. A frisson.

Hello, Isaac.

Blackout.

SCENE 2

Spotlight on Grace.

GRACE

I can't say I married for love. That's just something you get in
novels, I think. Oh, yes, I've read books. I've had schooling, I have.
I learned to read and write and do the counting. That came in
useful later on, too, the counting and accounting. Bookkeeping,
they call it. Keeping the books. Books of borrowing. Books of gold.
Was there a book of love? I don't know. This is Yorkshire; we
don't talk of such things. We try to do what is right, and in the end,
we do what we must.

My father owned Bell House at the time. The Hartleys had lived
there for years but William and Rosie were getting old, and when
she passed away, he couldn't run the smallholding and keep up
with the weaving, so there just wasn't enough coming in to pay the
rent.

It was my dad's idea. He wanted me off his hands, so he said he
would let William live at Bell House for free if one of his sons
would wed me. One mouth less to feed at home, and I would move
into Bell House to help the old man with the farm and the wool
work, so it would be good for everybody.

David was away in Brum, but Isaac was still at home, and we
courted for a while. He was more my age anyway, and I think we
could have been happy together. That might have been love; he
said he would do anything for me, and I believed him, at least for a
while, but that all changed when he had to marry Bessy, if you
know what I mean. Nobody ever said that life was simple.

I'm not going to miss the noise and bustle of the city, to tell you the truth. It was all right for a while, but this is where we grew up and this is where we belong. Moors and sheep, scrub and bracken, stones that twist your ankles and nettles that sting from a distance. And it's not as wet and grey as they say. Always rains in Yorkshire, the Brummies kept on saying. You don't want to go back there, they said. Last place God made, they said, and he was having a bad day at the time. Well, I don't mind somewhere quiet to bring up this one, if that's what it takes, as long as we've got a roof over our heads and food in our bellies. I can feel him kicking already. Must be a boy, the way he lashes out. And my David has never let us down. Oh, he has his ways, but he's been good to me, and I'm sure he'll be a good father. Or as good a father as any man can be that's got to fight and forage to make ends meet. That's what we've always done, our sort. Fight and forage. Fight and forage. Cradle to grave, blood to blood, dust to dust.

But look at me, getting all maudlin. This is my home now; we've left the heat and clamour of the land of iron and forges behind us and come here to this place near Cragg Vale in the Calder Valley, or just the Valley as David calls it. This is the earth we are forged from, and this is where we're going to start our new life. It's peace on the hillside from now on, and it's a bright new future we're going to stamp out for ourselves here, a glittering golden future in a bright new world.

SCENE 3

Bell House. The next day.

DAVID and ISAAC are sitting at the table. Each has a
tankard of ale.

ISAAC

So why did you come back?

DAVID

It was all arranged. You know that. Bell House belongs to Grace's
family.

ISAAC

Yes, but why now, with Grace in that state? I heard that you left
Brum because you had to.

DAVID

The less people know the better. But what I can tell you is that I
learnt a trade there.

ISAAC

I know. Blacksmith. Do you want to set up a forge here at Bell
House?

DAVID

Aye; I've got plans.

ISAAC

Plans?

DAVID

Plans for a better life. Look how Dad has aged. He can't carry on
like this any more. And you're working yourself to the bone for
nowt.

25

ISAAC

Well, there'll always be work for blacksmiths and the like, them as can work with iron. That's what Dad keeps saying, and he's right about that.

DAVID

I learnt other stuff, too.

Pause

ISAAC

I'm listening.

DAVID

You know how we used to, you know, bend the law a bit here and there?

ISAAC

Everybody does. A bit of thieving here and there. No harm in that. Some folks got more then they need and other folks are going hungry. That's just the way it is. And there's nobbut four officers for the whole of the Valley. And the nearest magistrate is in Bradford. And anyway, they can't hang you if they can't catch you.

DAVID

This is bigger than any of that. No more small stuff. We're going to be rich. I want you to get some of the lads together. Solid, reliable blokes who can keep their mouths shut.

ISAAC

This doesn't sound like blacksmith's work to me.

DAVID

Look out of that window. What do you see?

ISAAC

Sod all. Nothing for miles.

DAVID

Right. And you can see for miles. You can see if anybody's coming. So if they come, they'll never find anything. This is the perfect place.

Pause. ISAAC does not press for more. He just waits.

I'm going to set up a forge.

ISAAC

That's all?

DAVID

That's all. And I'll make bolts and buckles, hinges and brackets and stuff.

ISAAC

And that's all?

DAVID

Maybe not quite all.

DAVID takes a bright gold sovereign out of his pocket and hold it up to the light.

What do you think of this?

Blackout.

SCENE 4

Bell House. Several weeks later.

WILLIAM is seated, brooding. A dog barks.

WILLIAM

Is that you, our Isaac?

ISAAC enters through the front door.

ISAAC

Aye. Not at the loom, then?

WILLIAM

Can hardly see the threads any more.

ISAAC

You won't need to do that for much longer anyway.

WILLIAM

Wipe your boots when you come in here. It's filthy out there and this is a clean house.

ISAAC

Don't suppose our David's here, is he?

WILLIAM

No, he's been coming and going a lot lately. Might be back any minute, though.

ISAAC

Well, I might run into him on the way back, then. I just came to drop off some stuff.

WILLIAM

Stuff?

ISAAC

Tools and that. I've left them in the yard. I don't know where he wants them.

WILLIAM

What's it all for? Is this for his work? Building a smithy or something?

ISAAC

Something like that. I'd better get going. Tell our David I was here.

Exit.

WILLIAM

Will do.

WILLIAM settles down in his chair, dozes off. Time passes.

DAVID enters through the front door.

DAVID

(Jovial, ebullient)

Wakey, wakey! Come on, what's all this. Can't have you sleeping all day.

WILLIAM

Eh? What?

DAVID

Get that pot on the stove. A man needs something warm inside him on a day like this.

(Looking round)

Where's our Grace?

WILLIAM

Gone into Halifax. We've got to take the cloth to the merchants ourselves now. Gone on the cart with the folks from Lodge farm, and our Bessy's gone too, so she can be with Grace in case the baby's early.

DAVID

Well, we won't need to keep carting cloth into Halifax for much longer.

WILLIAM

What do you mean? You gonna start taking stuff into town? It's about time you got some work done. Been two months or so since you got back, and you haven't earned a penny as far as I can see.

DAVID

I'm not after the pennies, Dad. It's the big time I'm after. I've had enough of wearing rags and eating stale bread. Only the best from now on. Lap of luxury, that's what. I'm never going hungry again. You're gonna be proud of me when you're eating red meat every day and drinking the finest ale.

WILLIAM

I think you've been drinking too much already, that's what I think. You wasted your younger years hanging about with layabouts. Best thing I did was send you off to Brum to learn a trade.

DAVID

Yeah, yeah. Heard it all before. But that was the old me. This is the new me. I've got it all worked out.

WILLIAM

You've got sod all worked out. A dreamer that's what you are. All you've done so far is build a smithy in the back yard – not like any smithy I've ever seen, mind you. And you've earned nowt. All mouth and no trousers, that's what you are.

DAVID

You'll see soon enough. I've already started on a small scale. Testing the water, as you might say, and there's nothing to stop me. We're not going to be short of brass ever again. The money will come rolling in.

WILLIAM

I haven't seen you do a stroke of work here, you idle sod. All I ever see is you eating us out of house and home and surrounding yourself with lowlife, coming and going all hours and bringing the scum of the earth with you when you do show up.

DAVID

They're good lads. And I'm going to need them. And after a while, you won't even see them. I've been setting things up other places, too, but I'm gonna run everything from here. From Bell House. This will be our headquarters.

WILLIAM

Headquarters of what? You're off your rocker. You ain't got two pennies to rub together!

DAVID

No, I ain't got two pennies, but I got these.

DAVID empties a bag of gold coins onto the table. WILLIAM picks one up and studies it.

31

WILLIAM

What's all this? Where did you get all this gold?

DAVID

It's borrowed. But it will make us a fortune.

WILLIAM

Borrowed? Stolen you mean! No man gets this kind of money honestly. You've been doing Satan's work, you have, or you're the Devil himself.

DAVID

Not stolen, old man. Just loaned to me to turn into more. For hundreds of years, men have dreamed of making gold from next to nothing, and I know how to do it.

WILLIAM

Take it away. I don't want to know anything about it! Get it out of my house!

DAVID

Calm down. There's nothing wrong with it. These are real guineas, not clipped or coined or stolen. If a lawman walks into this house right now, there's nothing he can do but pat me on the back for being a good, law-abiding citizen.

WILLIAM

Ha! That'll be the day! You're a good for nothing layabout. Always have been.

DAVID

Just listen to me for a minute…

WILLIAM

I'm not having dirty money in my house and that's an end to it.

DAVID

There's no such thing as dirty money. There's money and there's no money and that's it. There's nowt else. It's summat or nowt. You want nowt? You've had it long enough and all you do is frigging moan.

WILLIAM

I brought you and your brother up to be clean, hardworking lads, not to go round thieving and clipping and threatening and bashing people's skulls in. You and your crowd are nowt but a bunch o' ruffians. You think you're so high and mighty because you've got a few bob, but you're just a lying, cheating, good-for-nothing useless arsehole. If I was a few years younger, I'd give you a good hiding right now. What would your mother say, eh? We scrimped and saved to send you off to learn an honest trade and you come back as feckless forger, faking when you could be working, throwing your lot in with a bunch of useless dickheads who haven't got half a brain between them. Thugs, that's all they are, and I don't want them in my house and I don't want you and your dirty business here either. Get out now before I…

DAVID

Before you what? Throw me out? Rat on me? Report me to the magistrate? You've got a hope. Who you gonna send as a messenger? Round here, it's what I say that goes. And I say we take control. There'll be clipping all over the valley from now on, but the wealth, the new money, our golden future, we create that here, in Bell House, where they can't get at us. And you can like it or lump it.

WILLIAM

When you set up the forge, I thought you were making bolts and hinges, stuff people need on the farms and in their homes, not melting down gold to make coins. That's counterfeiting, that is. You'll swing for it if they catch you. You'll end up rotting on Beacon Hill like a common criminal.

DAVID

Ah, no that's where you're wrong, you see. I'm way ahead of the game; I've thought it all through. Sit down and listen for a minute, will you?

WILLIAM sits.

Here, have some baccy.

DAVID hands over a pouch, which WILLIAM grudgingly accepts and proceeds to fill his pipe.

WILLIAM

You can't get round me with a pinch of baccy.

DAVID

Not trying to, Dad. Just want us both to calm down and have a nice little chat about things.

WILLIAM

Aye, well, you're not gonna change my mind about the clipping and forging. Counterfeiting the King's coins is a hanging offence. Everybody knows that.

DAVID

You're right there, Dad. And you know, I've always listened to you; always been a good son to you, haven't I? Even before I went away, I always saw you and Mum right, God bless her soul. I know it's always been backbreaking work at the loom, but I saw that you never went short. Others starved, but we always did all right. You've got to fend for yoursen round these parts. You always said so yourself.

WILLIAM

So what's changed? What are you getting at?

DAVID

Everything's changed, Dad. The old ways don't work any more. They're bringing in machines to do the weaving. They're building roads across the moors. People are leaving the land to go and work in Halifax and Bradford. The nobs and bigwigs don't care about us. Us farmers and weavers are going to starve if we don't take charge of our lives. That's what I learnt in Brummagem and thereabouts: that there's another way. And it's not about what we do; it's about how we do it.

WILLIAM

Sounds like daft talk to me – and what's that got to do with forging the King's guineas?

DAVID

It's called organisation, Dad. Doesn't matter what you do, as long as you're organised. As long as you've got a good bunch of blokes you can rely on. Lads who won't rat on you. Loyal people. Family.

WILLIAM

Family? We've got a family.

DAVID

We have, Dad, and you're the head of this family, and what you say goes. I understand that now.

DAVID pours WILLIAM a tankard of ale from a jug.

And that's why we won't do anything illegal.

WILLIAM

Nothing illegal? But I thought you said…

DAVID

I know… just a misunderstanding. You see, they passed a new law a while back. It's an offence to counterfeit the King's guineas. You're right about that, Dad. High treason, that is. I would never do that, never let that go on in this house.

WILLIAM

So what's all this about clipping and forging?

DAVID

We don't forge the currency of the realm. Ever. Only foreign coins. And that's not treason.

WILLIAM

You mean it's legal?

DAVID

A fine line, Dad, but believe me, they can't hang you for it. All I want to do is make a few Portuguese moidores. That doesn't do anybody any harm, does it? The King doesn't care. And if he did, there are no law officers for miles. And the local traders are all in favour. Nobody loses, Dad.

Pause. DAVID refills WILLIAM'S tankard.

WILLIAM

It sounds like a lot of trouble. Worse than that. It sounds like…

DAVID

.. change? Yes, you taught me that, Dad. If things don't change, they'll stay as they are. And they can't stay as they are, can they?

Pause.

Can they?

WILLIAM

I guess not. But this has always been a clean, God-fearing house. No laws have ever been broken in this house, neither God's nor man's.

DAVID

Nor will, they, Dad. I know how you feel about this house. We're setting up the forge out back, in a new building, walled off from the outside world. You won't even know it's there. And anyway, I need a forge for working with iron. That's what you want me to do, isn't it? Practice the trade I learnt? And Mum, who's looking down on us, will be smiling with that old sparkle in her eyes to know that we are doing well, that her sons have made good. And for Grace, now that she's so close to having a little one and won't be able to do much of the carding and spinning. She'll need time with the baby. She's been slowing down lately and sometimes just sits there and doesn't move, but she's so looking forward to being a mum, her face lights up when the little beggar kicks inside her. I think it gets to different women in different ways; sometimes she seems so sad, and then there are times when I think I've never seen her so happy. And I just want her to be able to take it easy and enjoy a new life.

37

WILLIAM

Well, if it's for Grace. If it will make her happy.

DAVID

I have to go now, Dad. Got to meet some people at Barbary's, do some organising. Set things in motion. There's good times ahead, Dad. Mark my words, you won't have to worry about a thing. We are going to rule the Valley from here. Now don't stay up too late, will you. I'll see you in the morning.

Exit DAVID.

WILLIAM

Rule the Valley? I thought it was for Grace.

Blackout.

SCENE 5

Spotlight on Grace.

GRACE

When it didn't work out with Isaac, I took off to join David in Brummagem. He was older than me, but we got on all right. He always talked about the future, about how he would provide for me, and we could raise a family, and isn't that what every girl wants. I say 'girl', but I was twenty-four at the time, so the sand was pouring faster and faster, wasn't it? I was expected to marry one of them, and David was nice enough, and well, it just seemed the right thing to do. David had a good job in the iron works. Hot, heavy work, it's true, but he's strong, our David, and not shy of hard work, so he did all right, brought home his pay quite regular.

But David learned another way to make a living, too, learned more than making bolts and hinges. There's lots of things go on in that part of the world, you know. Lots of things can be made of metal, if you know what I mean: things you can spend right away.

We lived in the beating heart of the unknown. Everything in life was an adventure: the vast human press of people in the city, the heat and clamour of the forges, the endless clatter of cartwheels on cobbles. We had started carving out a new life, engraving our world with symbols of dawning wealth, but it wasn't to last. Not there, not then.

Things took a turn for the worse in Brum, and William could no longer cope on his own, so we had to return to the windswept wastes of Erringden Moor. Shortly after we moved in at Bell House, David began sounding our neighbours out, and Isaac already knew who you could trust, who would have your back and who would stab you in it first chance they got.

Spring was in the air that day in 1767 when they came across the moor to Bell House. From Mytholmroyd they came, from Cragg Vale and Turvin, from Hebden and Heptonstall, from Luddenden and Sowerby. Word had gone round at Barbary's that something was afoot. But all in a whisper, just the trusted men: the strong and the good, they called them. They were certainly strong; they proved that.

SCENE 6

Bell House. A few days later.

DAVID, ISAAC and the COINERS are assembled around the table. GRACE, still pregnant, is serving bread and ale.

ISAAC

All right, lads, settle down. Most of you know why you're here and you all know you're here because you've proved yourselves in one way or another. You've either got the skills we need or you're ready and able to learn. And you're all here because you're trusted. Because I have vouched for you, or a loyal friend has sounded you out, or because our David has put you to the test in one way or another. But no word about any of this ever goes beyond these walls. Is that understood?

Murmurs

Is that understood?

Various affirmations of assent

I said, IS THAT UNDERSTOOD?

Loud cries of 'yes', 'aye', 'understood' etc.

So if any of you ever so much as breathes a word of what is said here today, you'll answer to the Hartleys. And you know what that means. You'll be scattered across the moor so fast and so far that they'll never find all the pieces. Understood!

Loud cries of support

Anybody want to leave before we get started? This is your last chance.

Silence

41

So I've done talking for now. It's over to our David. He's going to tell you how you are all going to be rich beyond your wildest dreams.

DAVID

Thank you, Isaac. Now lads, most of you know what the game is, but what you don't know is how we're going to make it work for real, how we're going to be rolling in gold before the authorities know what's going on and how we can keep on the right side of the law even if they start poking their filthy noses into our business. So let me set it all out for you.

You know the kind of life people have here in the Valley and on the hills, scraping a living out of muck and slime whilst King George and his acolytes down in London dine on goose liver and slurp down fine wines. How the cloth merchants pay us less and less for the weaving, so that folks are working day and night and yet still going hungry and burning their own cottages to keep warm in winter. Or having to choose between food and fire whilst there's others with more than enough, a hundred times more, a thousand times more. In the far-off capital, at the big trading centres, in the lush fields of the south, but not here in our gritty wilderness. They don't even know we're here, so it's down to us to put that right, to get it all level – to spread the wealth around a little. And here's the beauty of it all. This is not just for the weavers and farmers. It's for the good of all. Even the traders who have been short-changing the weavers for their cloth are going to be on our side. The innkeeper, the coachman, the artisan, they will all shower us with gold.

COINER 1

Gold? So that's it, is it?

DAVID

Well, you're no stranger to gold yourself now, are you, Sam? In fact, there's lots of folk here already clipped an odd coin now and again and it's always brought in a bit of income and never done anybody any harm, but nobody's ever really struck it rich. Why?

Pause.

I'll tell you why. No gold to clip. The likes of us don't often get our hands on nice fresh guineas in the first place. That's what's been holding us back. But not any longer.

COINER 1

So we steal it? But if we steal it, we don't need to clip it.

DAVID

No, if you steal it, you're going to get caught. We borrow it.

COINER 2

Borrow it? Who from? It's the traders, innkeepers, merchants and the like who buy and sell for gold. They're not going to lend us their money.

DAVID

They are. And do you know why? Because they will be greedy for more. We borrow their gold and pay them a nice fat rate of interest for their trouble. Nobody loses out.

COINER 3

We pay them more than we borrow?

DAVID

Listen. It works like this: We borrow a few guineas, clip off a bit of gold and trim the edges. We end up with the same number of guineas and a few clippings. Then we give them their guineas back

– full value to the naked eye AND half the clippings or coins to the value of half the clippings. Who do you know who's going to refuse a deal like that? And we keep half the clippings for melting down and striking into new coins at Bell House. I have the moulds for Portuguese coins and they are just as good as guineas nowadays. Believe me lads, once they've tried it out, lending us their guineas for a day or two, or even just an hour, they'll be back with more and the coins will come rolling in. And we'll keep proper records of the borrowings, proper ledgers with the incomings and the outgoings, so that everybody gets their fair share. It's all mapped out.

COINER 2

It's a hanging offence, that's what it is.

DAVID

Some say it is, and some say it isn't. Forging guineas is high treason, but forging Spanish or Portuguese money is misprision of treason. That's a much lighter sentence. But more importantly, they have to catch you first. And how are they going to do that? There are two constables for the whole of the West Riding and the nearest magistrate is in Bradford. And if they come, well, we can see them coming for miles. There'll be nothing for them to find.

COINER 1

What about them as don't want to lend us their gold?

DAVID

Well, it's early days yet, isn't it? But let's just say that we have to be prepared to persuade them, if you know what I mean. Any questions?

Silence.

44

ISAAC

Then I take it we are all agreed. We don't do voting here; we don't need to because we know what's what and we know who's who. They don't let us vote in parliament either, but that's probably a good thing because King George's barons and earls just tear one another apart. But George is not King here in the Valley. Only our David is King here.

(Raising his tankard)

To the King!

COINERS

To the King!

SCENE 7

Bell House. A few weeks later.

The loom has been pushed to one side. In its place is a workbench with metalworking tools and a balance.

ISAAC is weighing coins on the balance. DAVID enters from the yard. When the door to the yard is open, the glow from a forge can be seen. The farmyard noises are quieter than before.

DAVID

Are they full weight?

ISAAC

Some are, some aren't. It's getting hard to find coins that haven't already been clipped. And look at the state of these. Some of the men are just bringing in rubbish, anything they can lay their hands on.

DAVID

They're just keen, that's all. We've got over eighty collectors working as far afield as Todmorden and Boothtown and some stuff coming in from Bradford. Just make sure it all goes in the ledger. Grace can't do it right now.

Sounds of GRACE in labour from next room. They continue throughout the ensuing dialogue. Occasionally, BESSY'S voice can also be heard.

Anything that needs to go out?

ISAAC

(Indicating various bags of coins)

These ones go to Eastwood; this lot is for Sowerby, and I'll take these down to Barbary's myself. I've got to have a word with Jack Hardcastle. He's been having trouble at the Blue Boar.

DAVID

Trouble? What sort of trouble?

The landlord there is being difficult. Says the tax collector refused his money because it was under weight.

DAVID

(Laughing)

Fancy that! What a surprise.

ISAAC

Yes, nobody else has been bothered. Everybody round these parts is happy with the face value. A Portuguese moidore or a 4,000 reis coin has the weight stamped on it and that's what everybody accepts, but the taxman wants paying in guineas. A guinea is twenty-one shillings. You know that, I know that, everybody knows that, but it seems the taxman doesn't care about the face value. He just weighed a couple and said they were worth about seventeen shillings each. And if the gold weight is short, he won't take it at all. Can't pass it on to the Treasury in that state, he says.

DAVID

Well, it's been all right up to now. They've always been happy to fill their coffers with gold, any gold. London George is getting greedy. They've collected enough over the years. He's probably used it all up on his new carriage. The Gold State Coach, they call it. Seven thousand pound it cost, did you know that? Seven

47

thousand pounds for a fancy cart to pull him around in, and there's people starving all over the country.

Sounds from next door get louder. Clearly the baby is on the way.

Is this tax collector new?

ISAAC

It wasn't one of the usual minions. Big fellah. The Excise Supervisor himself, apparently. Man by the name of Dighton.

DAVID

Dighton? Yes, I've heard of him. Bit of a nuisance, if you ask me.

BESSY rushes in and out, fetching and carrying. She ignores the men.

ISAAC

So what do we do?

DAVID

Well, first of all, send Hardcastle back to the Blue Boar. Collect all the gold the landlord's got. Then we'll weigh it and pay him back in full-weight coins.

ISAAC

He won't like that. The face value will be less.

DAVID

Well, we're not going to give him a choice, are we? He's either with us, part of our family, or he's with them as wants to do us harm. His choice.

ISAAC

Right. We're just one big, happy family, we are...

Enter BESSY with baby.

BESSY

It's a boy!

DAVID

…and getting bigger all the time.

SCENE 8

Spotlight on Grace.

GRACE

So David and I came back to Yorkshire, to Bell House. We would have come back sooner or later anyway, because it was all agreed, but not when I was seven months gone with baby David. It was in Bell House that I first gave birth, and it was from Bell House that we changed the world, or our world at least.

And that's how it was. Not a great love story, you might think, but David's the man I married and gave myself to. Nobody forced me, but you have to be practical about things, don't you? And we were nothing if we weren't practical. But there were special moments, too, moments that came when you were least expecting them, moments that made your heart stop or leap with joy, moments that are burnt into my memory as if they were yesterday.

SCENE 9

Bell House. Three months later (Summer of 1766)

GRACE is seated at the workbench, counting coins and making entries in a ledger. DAVID enters through the front door.

DAVID

That dog's half asleep. Didn't even notice I was there.

GRACE

He knows you. He only barks at strangers.

DAVID

All the same, not much of a guard dog, sleeping during the day.

Pause.

Came across the top field. A couple of them ewes will be lambing soon.

Pause.

Are you all right, lass?

GRACE

You won't hear me complain.

DAVID

I know that. And I know it's been hard for you these last few weeks, what with the baby and all, but things are looking up. The new business is off to a good start, too. We're not going short any more, are we?

GRACE

Well, we've got enough to eat if that's what you mean.

DAVID

There's something, though, isn't there? Something bothering you?

GRACE

No, everything's fine. I've done the washing and the baking, and little David's having a nap. And the gold's all totted up. Do you want to see?

DAVID goes over to her and looks in the ledger.

DAVID

Are those the amounts for today?

GRACE

Yes, all up to date.

DAVID

Looking more closely. Is that today's date?

GRACE

I hope so; the ink's still wet.

DAVID goes back out through the front door. GRACE puts the coins and the ledger in a safe place and starts to lay the table.

After a moment or two, DAVID returns, holding a bunch of violets.

DAVID

Happy anniversary!

GRACE runs up to him and accepts the flowers. They embrace.

GRACE

Violets! My favourite. You remembered.

DAVID

I know I'm not much of a romantic, but …

GRACE

Shh…. Just hold me.

DAVID

I do love you, you know, Grace.

GRACE

I know.

DAVID

I might not say it often, but that's just not our way round here, is it? You know what I mean, we don't talk a lot in these parts. Always been too busy scraping a living.

GRACE

It's all right, David. But we'll have time from now on, won't we? Time for one another?

GRACE finds a vase for the flowers. DAVID goes to the bedroom door and holds out his hand.

DAVID

We have time right now.

GRACE takes his hand and follows him into the bedroom.

ACT II

(1768)

SCENE 1

1768. Two years have passed since Act I.

Spotlight on ANN.

ANN

I know what they say about them, that they are decent men who only clip the odd guinea to help the poor, to put food in their bellies and hope in their hearts, to make them feel valued and give them their dignity back. Hah! Not a bit of it! Liars and cheats, they are, thugs and ruffians to a man. Did I say man? Not a one of them is half the man my Robert is. And the women? Well, I suppose they have to put up with what they get. At least before all this villainy started, they could do some weaving. There's plenty of work at the loom around these parts, and the traders in Bradford and Halifax will always pay the best prices for a good piece of cloth. But now, they've forgotten all that; they're forced to live on their menfolk's ill-gotten gains, but they've still got mouths to feed, children to bring up, and old folks to look after. I'm not saying that they have easy lives, those that tend their farms and weave the cloth, but things were getting better before that monster came from the Midlands. Do you know, there's a man called John Kay invented a machine that will cut the weavers' work in half. The flying shuttle, it's called. Imagine that? It just flies from one side of the loom to the other like magic. And my Robert is helping the local traders to set up working palaces with dozens and dozens of looms where all the people can come together and enjoy the fruits of our modern lifestyle.

He's been good to me, my Robert and he's done so much good work in the town, the top solicitor for miles around, he is. Articled in Lincoln's Inn he was, before he came to Halifax to join our John's law firm. That's my brother-in-law, John Baldwin. He was struggling a bit at the time, but Robert put it all right. Hard work in chambers and cutting a fine figure in society, that's the key. I wouldn't say we were wealthy; I don't really think about it, but I admit that we're comfortable. Why only last week, we were dining with the Rawsons and Waterhouses, and it's done Robert's legal practice no harm that I'm a Prescott myself. Our names go a long way in this town: Robert Parker and Ann Parker, née Prescott. Well, you have to have connections if you're going to get on, don't you? And he's done so much good work for the community, my Robert. It's down to him that we got investors for the Turnpike from Halifax to Mytholmroyd.

It's an exciting time, a vital time in a vibrant town like ours and it quickens my heart to know that I'm at the centre of it, not just moving in society but helping Robert build a bright future for our citizens. We've got the best engineers, too. We've got none other than John Smeaton working on a water supply system for the town. Just think of that. Clean water delivered to every house. And there's talk of a man-made waterway, too, a canal that will speed up the movement of people and goods. What a future we will have! A clean, honest future for clean, honest, law-abiding citizens, people who don't rob and steal, but work hard and pay their way. And Robert's setting up a new court in Halifax to help traders collect small debts. Look after the ha'pennies and pennies and the shillings will look after themselves, that's what I was always taught. You mark my words, in a hundred years, people will look back on today and see it as a golden age for the Calder Valley, a golden age for Yorkshire, and a golden age for our great country.

SCENE 2

The Parkers' house in The Square, Halifax.

PARKER is seated. ANN enters, carrying a couple of hat boxes.

PARKER

Did you get what you wanted?

ANN

I've ordered some silks from Mr Spencer and found a couple of delightful hats at Mr Fuller's.

PARKER

That sounds splendid.

ANN

And Mr Spencer says that Lord Rockingham is back in town. Does that have anything to do with you?

PARKER

Yes, we're trying to get to grips with this coining business. Seems to be affecting everybody. He's going to write to London and demand action if things don't get any better.

ANN

Such a nice gentleman, Charles, I mean Lord Rockingham. My brother-in-law did some legal work for him when he was chief solicitor. That was before you came to Halifax, dear. We were invited to Wentworth House just before he became prime minister. A very able man, and such good manners. Perhaps we could dine together soon?

ROBERT

I'm sure we will. But don't forget, we're invited to the Dightons tomorrow.

ANN

Well, I hope they've got a new cook. Last time, the goose was definitely underdone. I didn't say anything, of course, because one doesn't, but she will have noticed what one left on the plate. It's her job to notice.

ROBERT

You are ever so slightly harsh, sometimes, my dear.

ANN

Not a bit of it! That meat was definitely pink, and the broccoli could have been firmer. I wouldn't stand for it here, you know that. I would give cook a piece of my mind.

ROBERT

I'm sure tomorrow will be fine. And William Dighton's a good friend; we don't want to upset anybody.

ANN

Don't worry, Robert. It's just that I like things to be right. You know that. But I know how to behave, you won't hear a thing from me, even if they thicken the sauce with sour cream and overdo the nutmeg.

ROBERT

All the same, it's nice of them to invite us and you got on all right with Ella last time.

ANN

Yes, William's very lucky. She's quite charming in her way, but somewhat reserved, I thought; rather aloof you might say, and she doesn't seem to give one her full attention at times.

PARKER

I'm sure we're all guilty of that occasionally, my dear.

ANN

I invited her to come along to our next literary soiree at Lady Henrietta's, but she seemed quite horrified at the idea. I don't think she gets out much.

PARKER

No, she has a certain strangeness about her. She prefers to stay indoors.

ANN

I would have thought that with all the children she's had, she would be glad to get out of the confines of the house now and again.

PARKER

I'm sure you're right dear. I have some work to do; I'll be in the study if you want me. Tell cook to ring when dinner's ready.

Exit.

ANN

She will. I wouldn't have it any other way.

SCENE 3

Meeting room at the Talbot Inn, Halifax.

*Various clergy, freeholders, merchants, business owners, etc.
are assembled for a meeting. PARKER is acting as chairman.
He strikes a gavel to call the meeting to order.*

PARKER

Gentlemen! As you are all aware, this meeting has been called to
enable us to discuss a number of pressing circumstances that affect
our community. My name is Robert Parker, Solicitor-at-Law, and I
have already had the privilege of representing some of you and
endeavouring to protect your interests in certain financial matters.

In that context, the first item on the agenda, is to relay to you, the
good citizens, producers, merchants and professional classes of
Halifax and neighbouring parishes, the latest information from His
Majesty's government pertaining to its proposed programme of
investment, opportunity and prosperity here in the West Riding of
Yorkshire and other areas of the country where regional
inequalities have resulted in stark disparities within the realm in
terms of economic expansion to the benefit of the worthy men and
women who contribute so effectively to the wealth of our nation.

CITIZEN 1

Contribute effectively? You mean we pay our taxes. We know we
do. Tell us something new!

PARKER

For that, let me hand you over to our distinguished guest here today,
for the gentleman you see to my right is none other than his
lordship the Marquess of Rockingham, who as I am sure you all
know, previously held the position of Prime Minister in his

Majesty's government and is now Lord Lieutenant of Yorkshire.
Could I please have a right Yorkshire welcome for His Lordship,
the Marquess of Rockingham.

Muted applause as ROCKINGHAM takes the floor.

ROCKINGHAM

Friends and fellow citizens of Yorkshire, let me first of all give you
a brief outline of the government's proposals for harnessing the
power of progress in our region. I have in my hand a letter from
Lord Weymouth, the Lord of the Treasury, setting out an ambitious
agenda for action in our area. The North of England is, in the
words of the noble lord, 'a fruitful oasis of enterprise, an Eden of
endeavour, indeed, a unique gem in the crown of our nation…'

CITIZEN 2

Bollerdocks!

PARKER

Sir! Please moderate your language!

CITIZEN 2

I'll moderate my language when he stops talking boll…

PARKER

I am warning you. I will tolerate no unrest in this chamber. My lord,
please continue with your deliberations.

ROCKINGHAM

I am merely reporting the contents of the documents sent to me
outlining the plans of His Majesty's government. Whilst I might
sympathise with the gentleman who interjected just now, may I
remind this assembly, that despite my own position, I am, in this
case, merely acting as a messenger. There is another business
which we shall come to in a minute, in which I may take a more

personal stance, but at the moment, I am passing on to you the wisdom of our present government, a wisdom which has been promulgated without my involvement. May I proceed?

PARKER

Please do so.

ROCKINGHAM

Then I will read the text of His Lordship's letter before we open the matter up for discussion.

CITIZEN 3

Why doesn't Weymouth come here himself and tell us what he has to say? I bet he couldn't even find Halifax on a map.

ROCKINGHAM

That is not for me to say. I merely quote from the missive in my possession: 'His Majesty's government is aware of the pressing need to improve the lot of our people in deprived and disadvantaged areas and is committed to the principle of creating a level bowling green throughout our great nation. This will mean improved transport routes so that goods can be moved more efficiently and at lower expense from their place of production to their required destination. This will benefit producer, merchant and the ultimate recipient, a boon to all concerned and in particular, a boost to the hard-working producers of worsteds and woollens as well as the clothworkers of our Northern Counties who toil so tirelessly for our common good.'

CITIZEN 1

Promises! Promises! We want action!

ROCKINGHAM

Please bear with me. I am simply quoting from the letter. Then we may hold an open discussion.

CITIZEN 2

We've heard it all before. New coach houses, cobbled roads all the ways from Leeds to Manchester. Rivers that run uphill. Never happens.

ROCKINGHAM

Finally, his lordship writes that 'Subject to certain provisions and on the presumption of proper and prior application, permission is hereby granted to press forth the progress of new transport routes across the Pennines by means of canal, turnpike or other innovation in order to facilitate and expedite the speedier passage of finished and semi-finished goods to their destination.'

CITIZEN 3

An up-and-over Pennine highway? Ha! They've been talking about that since Roman times. But it's all just talk. They're building palaces in London and highways to the southern coastline, but they don't care about folks in the Northern Counties. They want our cloth, but they don't want to help us deliver it. They're keen to tax our profits when we send the finest worsted abroad, but they're not going to help pay for its shipment.

ROCKINGHAM

Gentlemen, I am not part of the present government, but I can assure you that the watchwords of His Majesty's Westminster servants are 'professionalism, integrity and accountability' and I have no doubt that your concerns will be noted and passed on to the relevant department.

PARKER

At this point, I think we should adjourn for refreshments before we pass on to the next item on the agenda.

During the refreshment break, PARKER, ROCKINGHAM and DIGHTON go into a huddle in one part of the room, a number of citizens form a group elsewhere.

PARKER

I liked that bit about professionalism and integrity. From what I hear, the good Lord Weymouth spends more time gambling and carousing at White's than doing any government work.

ROCKINGHAM

Indeed. And that he has the King's favour has not prevented him from being royally lampooned in the broadsheets. But he's certainly accountable. He accounts for every penny he spends through his position at the Treasury.

DIGHTON

And yet we need his active support if we are to attract enough funds to clamp down on the criminal gangs that are causing havoc in this part of the West Riding.

ROCKINGHAM

Quite so. It is not our task here to question the wisdom of the present incumbents in London, but to get the good merchants of the West Riding on board our ship of action for the greater good, so that we may solicit their assistance in the matter of funding.

PARKER

It would be so much easier if Weymouth and the Treasury were on board too. After all, the yellow trade is to the detriment of the state and cannot be stamped out through will power alone.

DIGHTON

Perhaps, My Lord Rockingham, you could write to Weymouth to press that point home.

ROCKINGHAM

I fear that will have little effect. News of the Yorkshire coiners has already reached the Treasury, but it is considered to be a matter of little importance in the greater scheme of things.

CITIZEN 1

It's always the same. It's all right for King George to grant us permission to build all these new transport routes and 'promulgate the power of progress', but it's not the power we need, it's the money. The high-and-mighty in London are not going to pay for it are they?

CITIZEN2

Over sixty-four thousand pounds we invested in the Calder Navigation and what have we got to show for it? Nothing. Got as far as Brighouse before it all flooded, a few miles, that's all, and then it was wrecked.

CITIZEN 3

Well at least the turnpike to Mytholmroyd is open. That makes a difference.

CITIZEN 1

Not exactly a grand transport plan for the North, though, is it?

PARKER

Gentlemen, may we reconvene?

All resume their places.

The next item on our agenda is one which we have already touched on in the first half of this meeting, that of taxation. I have today heard many people quite rightly pointing out that our government's excise department is not without fervour in the matter tax collection. Now, that is not something I can influence…

CITIZEN 1

Nobody can!

PARKER

… but what I can influence is the fact that in recent months an increasing number of honest, upright businessman have been unable to pay their taxes in full because they found, upon doing so, that the gold they had set aside for the purpose does not have the value they had assumed. And unable to pay their taxes, they face prosecution, bankruptcy or both. In short, my friends, they find that their wings, like their guineas, have been clipped. Is this not so?

Muted expressions of agreement.

There is a rising scourge among us that started small but like the plague has grown to infect nearly every business and household in our otherwise prosperous, precious and pious parish of Halifax. We are upright god-fearing men who seek only to improve our lot and that of all honest, god-fearing citizens through industrious and righteous endeavour; we are law-abiding and loyal subjects of his majesty King George and we seek nothing but to retain the results of our labours, undiminished by the heinous machinations of malevolent miscreants. We are good citizens, true and loyal, are we not?

Murmured assent from those present.

And as loyal subjects, we the citizens of the West Riding of Yorkshire, know and understand, like all traders, landowners, craftsmen and wealth-makers the value not only of earning a guinea but of paying our way and making a fair contribution to the upkeep of services, the maintenance of law and order and the stamping out of evil criminality wherever we may encounter it. In this we are agreed, are we not?

Gentle murmur of assent from those present.

Are we agreed, gentlemen? Are we all agreed that we must stamp out the yellow scourge?

Stronger voices of agreement.

And that we will do whatever it takes to ensure that our revenues and taxes are not diminished by the evil that has descended among us?

Strong support from the citizens, cries of 'aye, whatever it takes', etc.

Let me therefore hand you over to a man many of you know already, Mr William Dighton, His Majesty's Supervisor of Excise, who will set out and propose for your approval the measures that have so far only been discussed behind closed doors for combating the present evil and restoring the values of justice, honesty and fairness to our civic landscape. Mr Dighton!

Dighton stands, is received with polite applause.

DIGHTON

Thank you, Mr Parker. As you know, my task in the parish of Halifax and beyond is to supervise the collection of levies due on local commodities such as cloth, beer and other forms of produce, such payment to be made in coins of verified value. Due to the actions of certain felonious counterfeiters, however, many coins offered to me in payment have been defaced and diminished to such an extent that I cannot accept them, leaving the otherwise honest innkeeper, trader or producer with an unpaid debt of significant proportion. As a result, Mr Parker here has been obliged to deal with numerous cases of bad debt and insolvency. I'm sure you agree with me that this has to stop.

The clippers live for the main part in isolated hamlets, homesteads and cottages, so that the chance of catching them red-handed is as remote as their farms on the moors. There is, however, another way to put an end to their illicit trade and that is by appealing to the very facet of their nature that set them on the path to perdition in the first place: their greed.

His Majesty's treasury already offers a considerable reward for information which will lead to the conviction of a murderer or highwayman, but the act of counterfeiting has attracted little interest. I therefore propose today, that just as local citizens and investors have succeeded in financing new transport routes and similar public amenities, it shall also fall to the citizens of the West Riding to cooperate in crushing the grip of the coiners and stamping out this yellow scourge.

CITIZEN 1

And what exactly does that mean?

DIGHTON

It means, sir, that we shall request and require a short-term financial contribution of one hundred guineas from each trader and business owner, such monies to be held in a fund reserved for the procuring of any information which successfully leads to a prosecution.

CITIZEN 2

And you think that will work?

DIGHTON

I am certain of it. They will smell gold. They will betray one another like rats. Greed is their motivation. Greed is their passion. And greed will be their downfall.

PARKER

The proposal is for a general per capita contribution of one hundred guineas to combat the counterfeiting. We will now take a vote. Is anybody against this motion to crush the criminals?

Silence.

PARKER

(With a resounding strike of a gavel)

The motion is passed!

SCENE 4

The Dighton's house in Bull Green, Halifax.

A middle-class domestic scene, which can be suggested with a minimum of furniture. The impression is that of a portrait pose of a happy family in drawing room, Ella Dighton seated with letter, dog at their feet, children, real or suggested, playing, drawing, sewing, etc.

ELLA

Cousin Jeb in Elland says that our John has been doing odd jobs for Mr Hargreaves the wheelwright and has been round to visit the Hargreaves at home a couple of times.

DIGHTON

Doesn't he have a daughter about the same age as our John?

ELLA

That's what I was thinking.

DIGHTON

Young love, eh?

ELLA

Could be. I haven't met her of course, but Jeb says she's presentable enough. John could do worse.

DIGHTON

Hargreaves might want a bit of a dowry, though. I just happen to know that he's having a bit of trouble paying his taxes.

ELLA

Trust you to think of that.

DIGHTON

Well, my work puts me in touch with people. That's not a bad thing, now, is it? Anyway, it might not be a bad idea to have a wheelwright in the family.

ELLA

Ha! Ha! You never know when a wheel's going to fall off your carriage!

DIGHTON

Keep your wheel rims clean and your axle shafts oiled, that's what my grandmamma always used to say.

ELLA

Really? Did she?

DIGHTON

Ha! Ha! Course not. She wouldn't know what an axle shaft was if she fell over one.

ELLA

Well, neither would I for that matter.

They laugh.

ELLA

Come on children, time for bed. Papa will come and read you a story in a minute.

DIGHTON

I have to go, out remember.

(To children, using a sock as a hand puppet)

Mr Socky is ever so sleepy.

Mr Socky says it's bedtime.

ELLA

Ooh, you are silly, sometimes. Mary!

Enter MARY, a servant.

It's their bedtime, Mary. Their father can't read to them tonight, but I'll be along in a moment.

MARY

Very good, ma'am.

ELLA

(To children)

Off you go, then. Papa will read to you tomorrow.

Exit MARY with children.

Do you really have to go out again? I worry so much.

DIGHTON

To Bradford. I might be gone a couple of nights. I have to collect some dues and then see the magistrate, Mr Leedes, about this coining business.

ELLA

Well, if you take a coach on the new turnpike, make sure the wheels don't fall off.

They laugh.

But seriously, promise me you'll be careful. I can't think what I'd do if something were to happen to you.

DIGHTON

Nothing's going to happen.

Exit.

SCENE 5

Bell House.

Subtle changes to the furniture and décor indicate the Hartley's growing wealth. Grace (heavily pregnant) is ironing and folding clothes. She is simply dressed, but her clothes are smarter than before. Her bonnet is new.

Bessy enters through the front door. She is well dressed and carrying a basket laden with food.

GRACE

(Indicating Bessy's dress)

Well, well, look at you!

BESSY

(Giving a twirl, showing off her dress)

Best Manchester cotton from Mrs Aston's haberdashery. I had it made up by Nora Whiteley in Halifax.

GRACE

Do you think people notice?

BESSY

Notice what?

GRACE

That things are getting better for us. That we're quite comfortably off, now.

BESSY

I hope so. Not much point in buying new clothes otherwise, is there? Why?

GRACE

It's just that sometimes I worry that it's all too much, too soon. When I go down to the village or into town, I can feel people looking at me, like they can see the difference. I mean folks I've known all my life, from before I went away. I don't feel like I'm one of them anymore.

BESSY

That's because they look up to you now. You're King David's wife. That means something.

GRACE

Don't say that. I don't want to be just thought of as somebody's wife. I'm somebody in my own right, not just a washing, cooking, baby-making machine for my husband.

BESSY

I know, but that's just the way it is. Maybe it'll all change one day, and we'll have a woman prime minister. Then she'll lay down the law and make men and women equal before you can say Jessie Bunny Rabbit.

GRACE

Hah, they'd have to let us vote, first. Even most of the men can't vote.

BESSY

No, you have to own land and property and all that. Well, maybe one day.

GRACE

But it's not just that, Bessy. I'm worried that if people begin to notice, they might start to ask questions and I'm not sure if that's a good thing. People asking questions. The wrong sort of people, I mean.

BESSY

Nah, you worry too much. Things are fine just as they are and getting better every day.

GRACE

(Indicating the basket.)

Been to market, too, I see.

BESSY

A joint of beef and nutmeg to go with it. Oranges and lemons, and grapes from a travelling trader. When did we ever have the likes of them before? It's our time, now, Grace. We owe it to ourselves, don't you think?

GRACE

I suppose so. I could do with some more help around the house, though. The menfolk had little enough time before. I hardly see our David for days on end nowadays and when I do, he's at the forge most of the time. But I guess that's the price we have to pay for our new lifestyle. The men have important work to do.

BESSY

Some do, I dare say. I think my Isaac's getting lazier every day.

GRACE

Don't say that. I'm sure he's got a lot on his mind. He's got a lot of responsibility.

BESSY

As second fiddle to your David, you mean? Sometimes I think that's what's bothering him. They don't seem to get on that well any more.

GRACE

They're brothers. That's what brothers are like. David works hard, but he couldn't do it without your Isaac. That's why they call Isaac the Duke of York.

BESSY looks around mock-furtively.

GRACE

It's all right. There's nobody to eavesdrop. Except baby David, and he's fast asleep. A real nuisance when he's awake, though. He'll grow up to be as headstrong as his father one day.

BESSY

You know what you were saying about the men doing the important work?

GRACE

Well, they do. Men and women are just the same, really. Some work till their hands and feet are red with sores, and others are bone idle and do sod all, men or women. It's just that we have different jobs on the farm, different things to do around the house. The way things were before, the women did the spinning, and the men did the weaving, and now, something else has taken over from the weaving.

BESSY

I know: the clipping. It's the same all over the valley. Do you know what the difference is between a man and a woman?

75

GRACE

No, what?

BESSY

The WOMAN cleans the house, feeds the children, feeds the pigs and feeds the chickens, collects the eggs, picks the vegetables, plucks a goose…

GRACE

(Getting the idea)

…gets the wool in, spins the yarn, prepares the food, cleans the table, stokes the fire, brews the ale, sets the table, pours the drinks and serves the food…

BESSY

…washes up, clears the bench, lays out the tools, positions the chair, takes the coin from its hiding place…

GRACE

…enters the value into the ledger…

BESSY

…and then – and this is the REALLY IMPORTANT THING, because this is what brings in the money and keeps us all in the lap of luxury with so much leisure time to enjoy…

BESSY and GRACE

(Together)

…THE MAN CLIPS THE COIN!

They both burst out laughing.

GRACE

And then it's off to bed.

BESSY

Just one chore after another, ha ha!

GRACE

All the same, if David hadn't taken control, we'd be no better off than anyone else. If it weren't for the clipping, the whole valley would starve, but it still wouldn't be enough because the gold always had to be passed on to people who would take the lion's share and would cheat you out of the rest, given half a chance. Everybody is doing the clipping, but it's only here in Bell House that good quality coins are made.

BESSY

(Indicating a pile of clothes that need folding.)

Here, let me help you with that.

(They set about folding bedsheets.)

You know you were saying that you could do with more help around the house?

GRACE

Well, there's always so much to do, and when you're starting a family as well…

BESSY

I have an idea. You know my cousin Edie? The one that lives over on Moorside Farm?

GRACE

The one that's a bit… different?

BESSY

They say she's no use on the farm, but she could make herself useful here.

77

GRACE

I couldn't pay a wage.

BESSY

Well, you could. But you wouldn't have to. How about board and lodgings in return?

GRACE

That might work.

BESSY

And a bit of pocket money, I suppose. To be honest, I think she'd be glad to get away from the clutches of certain farmhands, if you know what I mean. She's just at that age.

GRACE

I'll think about it.

(Baby cries.)

I wondered how long the peace would last.

Exits to bedroom.

BESSY

(Picking up a pile of laundry and following her.)

I'll get the beds made.

Exit.

SCENE 6

Bell House. Several weeks later.

Grace is seated, feeding her new baby. Edie enters from the yard. Edie has a visible disability. When the door to the yard is open, farmyard noises can be heard.

EDIE

When will the Master be back?

GRACE

Do you mean my husband, King David?

EDIE

Yes, Missus Grace, but he said not to use that name at home. It's sort of a secret word so that others can talk about him without using his real name, in case anybody is listening. So I just call him 'Master' because that's what he is to me. And anyway, he's not a real king, is he? Doesn't have a crown or anything.

GRACE

You watch what you're saying, young Edie! I took you in to save you from rolling about in the muck with the ruffians down on Moorside, but I can just as soon send you back to wallow in the bog you came from.

EDIE

But then you wouldn't have nobody to fetch and carry for you when you can't do it, would you? Nobody to feed the animals or stop young David crying when you're having a lazy turn.

GRACE

What do you mean? I haven't got a lazy bone in my body! Always at it, I am, morning noon and night. I'll make you wash your mouth out with pigswill if you talk like that.

EDIE

Whatever you say, Missus Grace, but folks say you've been different ever since the baby was born.

GRACE

Stop talking nonsense.

EDIE

So when will he be back?

GRACE

He'll be back when it suits him. Like you say, he's the Master. Why?

EDIE

We have to move the chickens. There's no room for them out back with the new forge. I can't do it on my own. We'll be having roast chicken every day if we don't do something.

GRACE

Well, you'll just have to find other stuff to do till he gets here, won't you? Here, put this one to bed.

GRACE hands the baby to EDIE.

EDIE

Yes, Missus Grace.

Exit to bedroom. GRACE remains seated.

Blackout.

SCENE 7

Scene: the same. The following week.

The sound of hammering and forging from off. Flame effects visible when the yard door is open. There are no farmyard noises.

The loom stands to one side, disused, its place taken up by a workbench. Metalworking tools hang in place of shuttles and thread. On the bench are some suspicious-looking clipping tools and a stack of gold coins. GRACE is weighing and counting coins and making entries in a ledger.

David enters from the yard and adds a number of coins to the stack.

DAVID

We're nearly done for today. How's it looking?

GRACE

Fifteen percent up on last month so far, thanks to the trouser makers in Mytholmroyd. If they do well, we do well.

DAVID

Like I always say, everyone's a winner.

EDIE enters from the bedroom.

EDIE

The baby's asleep and I've tidied up and put all the clothes away.

GRACE

Right. Go and scrub the front steps, then you can sweep the back yard when the men have gone.

EDIE exits via the front door.

The noises from the yard stop. ISAAC and BROADBENT enter from the yard.

ISAAC

David, where did you put the other dies?

DAVID

I'll get them in a minute.

BROADBENT

(Looking at the gold on the bench)

So where's my share?

ISAAC

You get yours when it's all totted up at the end of the week, Jim. You know that.

BROADBENT

Yeah, but it never seems to amount to much, looking at what you've got here.

DAVID

That's not our gold, you dimwit. That's what we owe to them as we borrowed from.

BROADBENT

All the same...

DAVID

Are you accusing me of something, James Broadbent?

BROADBENT

No, I'm just saying, I could do with a bit now, up front, like. I've been having a bit of a hard time lately and you seem....

ISAAC

Let it go, Jim. You'll get your share. Everybody gets a fair share. But nobody gets favours, all right?

DAVID

Come on, you two, we've still got work to do.

The three men go back out into the yard. The hammering and clanking noises start up again.

GRACE

(To herself)

All this bickering. They never used to be like that. Like children, they are sometimes.

EDIE comes hurrying in through the front door.

EDIE

They're coming!

GRACE

Who is?

EDIE

Them. Doesn't matter who. If I don't know them, they're strangers – and the Master said strangers are trouble.

GRACE

(Opening the back door and shouting though to the yard.)

David!

The clanking and hammering falls silent. David appears in the doorway.

Edie says someone's coming.

83

DAVID

Right.

(Shouting out to the back)

They're on the way! You all know what to do!

He sweeps the gold coins and clipping tools into a box and takes them out back, returns and picks up some iron working tools at the workbench and starts to gently tap at some iron work, humming or whistling cheerily as he works. GRACE and EDIE clear away a few signs of affluence and busy themselves with cooking and housework. Taken together with the children, the overall effect is of an industrious rural craftsman and his family going about their everyday lives.

A dog barks. There is a knock at the door. GRACE opens without delay. The bailiffs force their way in, followed by Dighton. GRACE smiles at them innocently.

GRACE

Good morning, gentlemen. What can I do for you?

Dighton and the bailiffs stomp around, poking at things and assessing the situation.

DAVID

Holding up a door bolt he has been working on.

Can I interest you in a bolt for your stable door, sir?

Dighton and David come face to face and square up in enmity.

Nothing to see here, officer. You'd best be on your way.

Dighton backs down and heads for the door.

DIGHTON

I'll be back.

Dighton storms out in anger, followed by the bailiffs.

DAVID

Like hell you will!

GRACE

A bolt for your stable, door! Ha, ha, ha!

All roar with laughter.

Curtain.

ACT III

(1769)

SCENE 1

August 1769. A year has passed since Act II.

Bell House. Grace is pregnant with her third child.

DAVID and ISAAC are at the workbench, clipping coins.
BROADBENT is fetching and carrying things from the yard.
GRACE is preparing food, chopping fresh vegetables etc.
WILLIAM enters through the front door.

DAVID

Been out, have you?

WILLIAM

Aye, tha knows where I've been. You should have come too. All of you.

ISAAC

To see the preacher man, you mean?

WILLIAM

Aye, to hear Mr John Wesley, speaking at Hoo Hole farm. Hundreds of folk there, there was. Never heard anything like it. Got the fire of God in him, Mr Wesley, has.

DAVID

We got the only fire we need right here in Bell House. Fire for the furnace to melt the gold, fire for the pot to cook our food, fire to put fear in them as gets in our way.

WILLIAM

That's heathen, talk, that is! That's Satan's fire you're playing
with! This has always been a good, honest, God-fearing house, this
has. It's the Bible we should be living by, not your borrowing
books for clipping and coining. You could do worse than listen to
Mr Wesley's warning. I could feel it when he spoke, everybody
could, a simple choice: God and salvation or Hell fire and
damnation.

DAVID

Got work to do, old man. No time for rich, loud-mouthed preachers
and all their talk.

WILLIAM

'Whosoever has food to eat, and raiment to put on, with something
over, is rich.'

DAVID

Preachers don't put food on the table; only gold does that.

WILLIAM

'A thousand pound supplies the want of twenty thousand qualities.'

DAVID

Keep it to yourself!

WILLIAM

'It's a deep gulf of temptation into which you have fallen, a
temptation out of which nothing less than almighty power can
deliver you.'

DAVID

I'll show you almighty power if go on like that.

WILLIAM

'As money grows, so the love of money grows; it increases in the same proportion.'

DAVID

Stuff it in your pipe. I've got mouths to feed.

WILLIAM

It's gone beyond feeding mouths with your lot. You're never satisfied. You don't know when to stop.

Pause.

I've been talking to folks.

DAVID

Oh, aye? And what do these 'folks' say?

WILLIAM

Some's afeared to talk, and others talk too much. There's them as are happy to hand coins over for clipping and get a fair return, but there's them that only do so 'cos they're afeared of a beating or worse if they refuse. And there's them who've taken a beating or had stuff happen to their families.

DAVID

None o' your business, old man. You just keep outa stuff that don't concern you!

WILLIAM

Show some respect, or I'll…

DAVID

(Squaring up to face WILLIAM)

Or you'll what?

WILLIAM

Oh, you're a big man, now, are you? Fight with an old man, would you? Well, I can still show you a thing or two. And I can still throw you out of here. This is MY home, promised to me! Go and get your own place if you want to be so high and mighty, Mr King David!

GRACE

Stop it, both of you! You're like a pair of overgrown children! As if there aren't enough babies in the house already!

DAVID

You keep out of it!

Sound of a baby crying.

Get the hell out of here, go look after your brat!

Exit GRACE to bedroom.

WILLIAM

I'm just saying, you should have gone to see Mr Wesley. He's a great man; he knows what's right and what's wrong: 'Riches have increased with thee; at the peril of thy soul. Set not thine heart upon them!'

DAVID

Oh, go fling your flagon!

DAVID rushes off through the front door.

WILLIAM

(Shouting after him)

You stupid young lump o' sodgrass.

ISAAC

Let it go, Dad. David's right. We haven't got time for this. We've got work to do, stuff to deliver.

(To BROADBENT)

Pack that stuff together and bring it to Barbary's.

Exit.

BROADBENT

You shouldn't get upset, Mr Hartley. David's only doing what he knows.

WILLIAM

That's as may be, but he'd better watch out. There's a fellah from over Halifax way that's out to get them as is doing the coining.

BROADBENT

What fellah?

WILLIAM

Man called Dighton. They say he'll pay good money for information.

BROADBENT

Information?

WILLIAM

Information about the clipping.

BROADBENT

And then what?

WILLIAM

Oh, take no notice of me; it's all just talk.

BROADBENT

What is it they want to know?

WILLIAM

Not for me to say. I'd never talk to nobody about nothing. I don't want anybody to come to any harm, and I would never betray my own, but this coining has to stop. I just want things to be like they were, or better; but not worse, not satanic. Good honest work is what made us what we are. Farm and forage, crop and cut, comb and card, weft and warp, but not … not this way. … The yellow way is foreign. It's not our way. It's not God's way.

BROADBENT

So you think somebody should do something?

WILLIAM

I'm not saying that. Every man has his own conscience. Every man knows what is right. Right for him and his family.

BROADBENT

Nobody here would do it. None of us in the Valley would ever talk to the taxman.

WILLIAM

I know. Nor I. I would never betray my own.

BROADBENT

We're all loyal folk here. Loyal to King David, your son. Nobody would ever say anything against him.

WILLIAM

Course not. I wouldn't expect them to. Not for a hundred guineas.

BROADBENT

Is that what they're offering?

WILLIAM

That's what they say, a hundred guineas. But like I say, it's all just talk. I would never betray my own. I would never want anybody to do anything like that. I just want the coining to stop.

91

SCENE 2

Parker's Law Chambers. One month later.

Parker and Dighton are seated side by side behind a desk, tribunal fashion. In front of the desk is a single, hardback chair.

PARKER

Are you sure this man is ready to talk? Can we trust him?

DIGHTON

He's a bit of a rough diamond. Well, actually more a rough lump of millstone grit, but yes, he's ready to squeal. Maybe he's had a bit of a set-to with David Hartley and thinks he can mix revenge and profit by pointing the finger. It's the lure of gold. It infects their reason and drives them mad.

PARKER

But can we trust him?

DIGHTON

Can we trust a proven villain who is already known to be a liar and a cheat? I'd say you can trust him as far as you can pay him. A hundred guineas can buy a lot of trust.

PARKER

A hundred guineas!

DIGHTON

If necessary, it will come out of the fund. We have already started collecting from the community. Let this be a test case for our new approach to this problem. And it will be worth it to put an end to this yellow scourge.

Enter SERVANT.

SERVANT

There's a Mr Broadbent to see you, sir.

PARKER

(To DIGHTON)

Well, let's see what he has to say.

(To SERVANT)

Show him in.

SERVANT admits BROADBENT, then leaves.

Welcome Mr Broadbent. Take a seat.

BROADBENT sits uncomfortably.

BROADBENT

Thank you, sir.

PARKER

Now, let's not waste time. You know why you're here. It's because you have certain information that you are prepared to disclose. Is that right?

BROADBENT

Yes, sir.

PARKER

And it concerns illegal activities that you have personally observed. Is that not so?

BROADBENT casts a look at DIGHTON and remains silent.

Mr Dighton here is from His Majesty's Treasury. He is familiar with the case and needs to hear what you have to say.

93

BROADBENT

I said I would tell you what I know, sir, there was no mention of anyone else.

PARKER

Come, man. Your statement will become public knowledge. It needs to be brought before the court. You must testify that you have personally witnessed the clipping of His Majesty's legal currency.

BROADBENT

I'm saying nothing till I've had the reward I was promised.

PARKER

Mr Broadbent, let me lay out the facts as I understand them. ONE: you have already admitted to being a member of the coiners' gang, that you have personally been present during the clipping of the King's guineas and the forging of certain gold coins. On my evidence alone, you can be taken to York tomorrow and held there until the Spring Assizes. It will only take a word from me, and you will never see the Calder Valley again. TWO: Notwithstanding the aforegoing and undisputed fact, you are willing, in exchange for a Tyburn ticket, which will excuse you of certain duties and obligations, to implicate certain other persons in the act of counterfeiting, and THREE: It is agreed that, subsequent to your testimony in court, you will receive a handsome payment for the valuable assistance you have rendered in securing certain convictions. Do you agree that the salient facts of the case pertaining to your own position are precisely as I have outlined them?

BROADBENT

I... suppose so.

PARKER

Then you will be paid a suitable sum after you have testified.

BROADBENT

A hundred guineas.

PARKER

Mr Dighton, can the Treasury accede to a demand of this magnitude?

DIGHTON

On my authority, I will advocate the case for such magnanimous generosity.

BROADBENT

Does that mean 'yes'?

PARKER

Mr Broadbent, you shall have your due compensation as agreed in return for your testimony, provided that you identify a certain David Hartley as one of the men you saw clipping the King's coin.

BROADBENT

I'm not going to York! I'm not going to court! Ever! *(Stands.)* The deal's off!

DIGHTON

(Soothing)

Come now, Mr Broadbent, don't be so hasty. There is another way.

BROADBENT sits.

You don't need to go to York. We will take you to the office of Mr Leedes, the Magistrate in Bradford, and there you can make a statement implicating David Hartley in the act of counterfeiting and put your mark on a paper to that effect. Then your part in the business is done. Do you agree?

BROADBENT

And then I get my money?

DIGHTON

Once you have made your statement in front of the magistrate, I will ensure that you receive...

PARKER

Do you agree, man? Yes or No. If you have come to waste our time, you can get out now!

BROADBENT

All right, then. Yes, I agree. A hundred guineas?

DIGHTON

You will receive your reward as soon as you have identified David Hartley before witnesses.

BROADBENT

No! I'm not doing that! He'll kill me!

PARKER

He won't have a chance. He'll be banged up in gaol before he knows who pointed the finger. Will you do it?

BROADBENT

No! Never!

DIGHTON

Mr Broadbent, listen to me. You will do it. For two reasons: Firstly, if you do not do as we say, we will release word of your presence here, and your fellow coiners will draw their own conclusions from your agreeing to meet with us here. And secondly, and I hope you will appreciate my kindness and generosity in this, I will DOUBLE THE REWARD paid from the King's coffers by adding the same amount out of my own purse. Now, one last time: Do you agree?

BROADBENT

Two hundred guineas?

DIGHTON

Double the amount previously agreed. You have my word.

PARKER

Stop wasting our time, man. DO YOU AGREE?

BROADBENT

Yes, I agree.

PARKER and DIGHTON stand. BROADBENT is obliged to follow suit.

PARKER

Thank you, Mr Broadbent. We know where to find you. We will send word and tell you when and where we require you to appear.

BROADBENT

Thank you, sir.

Exit.

As Broadbent leaves, the two men sit and breathe a sigh of relief.

PARKER

That was a bit over the top, don't you think. Saying you'll double the reward.

DIGHTON

Not really.

PARKER

You mean…

DIGHTON

Firstly, he is a villain and a traitor and deserves everything that's coming to him, and secondly, I only said I would advocate the case for generosity, not that the reward would be granted. The devil, Mr Parker, is in the detail.

PARKER

Ha! Ha! Ha! The devil indeed!

SCENE 3

Bell House.

GRACE, still pregnant, is rocking a crib holding Mary, now 18 months old. WILLIAM is sitting by the fire, reading the Bible. DAVID is whittling a piece of wood.

GRACE

(Singing softly to Mary)

> Sleep, baby, sleep,
> Thy father guards the sheep,
> Thy mother shakes the dreamland tree,
> And from it fall sweet dreams for thee.
> Sleep baby sleep.
> Thy father guards the sheep.

DAVID

(In a good-natured, jocular fashion)

Ha! Ha! Can't be bothered with sheep nowadays. Got other things on my mind.

WILLIAM

Aye, well, that used to be our way of life. Sheep is what these hills were made for.

DAVID

Things have changed, Dad.

WILLIAM

'And when he hath led forth his own sheep, the sheep follow him, for they know his voice.'

99

GRACE

I think she's nodded off. We'll have a bit of peace for a while.

> *(To David)*

What are you making?

DAVID

A spinning top for young David. Where is he anyway?

GRACE

He's in the nursery. Oh, doesn't that sound posh? Nursery? Who ever thought we'd be using words like that?

> *EDIE enters from the bedroom.*

EDIE

Young David's asleep. I'll just see to the dog, then I'll be off to market.

GRACE

No market this time of day, but it wouldn't surprise me if the miller's boy is down at the marketplace, and you might accidentally bump into him. Anyway, don't be gone too long. It gets dark early at this time of year, and I'll need your help with a few things later on.

EDIE

No fear, missus Grace. It'll be all sheep and no wolves till I get back.

> *Exit.*

DAVID

She's really shaping up, that lass. You've done wonders for her since she's been here.

GRACE

She certainly knows her own mind and she's been a great help around the place.

DAVID

I have to be getting along, soon, too.

GRACE

(To David)

Will you be out late out tonight?

DAVID

Might be. We're having a bit of a 'do' at the Old Cock in Halifax.

GRACE

In Halifax? Why not at Barbary's? That's our local. That's where everyone is trusted, you've said so yourself often enough. And from what I hear, the lawmen have been snooping around again, and some men have been arrested.

DAVID

Only idiots and weaklings and them as can't look after themselves. Idiots are arrested many times before they die. The clever are only caught alone. And I'm never alone; the lads have got my back.

GRACE

All the same, you have to be careful. Halifax is beyond the Valley.

DAVID

I know, but that's where a lot of our business is now, and it's three years since we started out, so today's a bit special; it's time to give the lads a dollop of encouragement and keep their spirits up.

GRACE

Well, just be careful, that's all. I'm so happy that we've landed on our feet here. I don't want you taking any risks. 'Love all, trust a few, do wrong to no-one,' someone once said.

DAVID

Not so sure about the 'love all' bit, but don't worry, lass. Everything will be all right. I'll be back before you know it.

    Exit.

SCENE 4

A tavern (The Old Cock, Halifax). Saturday, 14 October 1769.

One or two locals are seated SR, away from the main door.

Enter DIGHTON and PARKER from the street SL.

DIGHTON

This is where he'll be. He thinks he's safe here. Amongst his men. Thinks they're his subjects and he's untouchable. Well, now that we've got evidence against him, he's going to find that he isn't as high and mighty as he thinks. I've got a warrant from Mr Leedes in Bradford and he's sending bailiffs to help get the job done. We'll clap that rogue Hartley in irons before he knows what's happening.

PARKER

And I'll be your witness to any resistance or violence from his men. If they try to obstruct the law, they'll have to answer to me, and the good citizens of Halifax that I represent.

DIGHTON

No, I need you as a witness to the identification, nothing more, and we are beholden to keep the local dignitaries out of it. This action is by order of the Marquess of Rockingham, but it's strong-arm stuff. It could be a nasty business and we don't want anyone taking revenge later. I have men watching for the miscreant to show his face and when he does, we will be back to see that justice is served and that this noble borough is freed from this malevolent menace once and for all.

PARKER

And you reckon nabbing Hartley will put paid to the whole business?

103

DIGHTON

The coiner's mob is a craven cur, violent and aggressive, but not without cunning. Half dog, half fox, you might say, but cut off the head and the beast dies. Hartley has gone over the top by declaring himself King of the Valley. If he falls, they all fall.

PARKER

I hope you're right. It's all gone on long enough and it's the honest, hard-working traders who suffer. Decent men who've been cheated by the clipping and can't pay their taxes with underweight guineas and forged moidores. It's hurting trade in the Valley and it's hurting the nation's coffers. They've made a cesspit out of honest endeavour.

DIGHTON

Let's get out of here. I can't even stand the smell of the place.

Exit DIGHTON and PARKER through main door to street.

SCENE 5

Scene: the same. Later the same day.

Lights go up to reveal coiners seated seats at the table furthest from main door, prominent amongst them DAVID. Raucous singing and carousing in progress). No shortage of serving girls and female companions.

COINER 1

Sing us another one…

COINER 2

How about this?

(Sings)

There was a young fellah from Hebden…

COINER CHORUS

Hebden!

COINER 2

Who shagged a young lassie from Diggel…

COINER CHORUS

Diggel!

COINER 2

They rolled in the clover

COINER 3

But she chucked him over

Expectant pause.

COINER 4

And now he's short of a wiggle!

COINER CHORUS

And now he's short of a wiggle!

Laughter and merriment all round.

ISAAC

A toast!

COINERS

A toast!

ISAAC

Raise your glasses to the man who filled them for you! The man who brought the good life to the Valley. The man whose skill, courage and determination has freed us from the yoke of absent rulers and thieving London aristocrats. To our leader and true sovereign, King David Hartley. The King!

COINERS

The King! Speech! Speech!

ISAAC

(To DAVID)

You'd better say a few words. They know this is the best life we've ever had, but they want to hear it from you.

DAVID

It's been three years now since I came back to the place of my birth, and in that time, we have built up a life for ourselves, we have risen out of the shit and muck the landowners and merchants had covered us with. We can all stand proud that we have taken control of hill and dale, that we can live without fear, without going hungry. We have found our own way, the way of the Valley, the new way, not for ourselves, not for riches or gain, but for our families, for our childer and for our old folk, so that we can feed them and clothe them and give them back their dignity. We are proud men of the Valley. Are we not?

Coiners shout out their support and clatter their tankards.

What are we?

Shouts of 'proud men of the Valley' Even louder shouts of support and clattering of tankards.

And we are good men. Loyal and true. What are we?

COINERS

Loyal and true!

DAVID

I thank you my friends from the very depth of my soul. This has always been my dream: to have men about me who are true, solid, stable men who swear the loyal oath. This is why there is no way they can touch us.

The London King and his cohorts don't look after us. They keep all their money in the south and don't care about ordinary folks here in the hills and valleys. It's like they don't even know we are here. We have to fend for ourselves and look after our own, and that's what we, my gallant band of brothers, have been doing. One day there will be a golden age when we all are treated equally throughout the land, but this is OUR golden age. Right here. Right now!

Cheers of support.

The puny pathetic parrots of the marquess and his minions can never break the hearts of folk forged of millstone grit. This is our

107

land, this is God's own country, these are the hills and valleys that
bore us. This is where we belong, and they have no place. If they
come, we will fight. If they try to destroy our living, we will
defend our birthright. We will stand up for what is right. We will
stand against oppression. We will stand together. Never again will
we suffer their evil…

Enter DIGHTON, PARKER and BROADBENT.

DIGHTON

(At the top of his voice)

Silence!

Murmurs, laughter, catcalls, but then the coiners fall silent.

I come in the King's name!

Laughter and defiance from coiners.

COINER 1

Which king? This is our King.

DIGHTON

That man is no king! He is a ruffian and a rogue, a criminal and a
cut-throat. As are many of you. But you are safe. He is the only one
I have come for. Give him up and you will all be safe from the law.

Cries of 'Never!' etc. from the coiners.

DAVID

You have no business here, tax man, and no authority. Be gone
before you regret speaking words that could be your last.

DIGHTON

Mr Broadbent, you told me that you saw a certain man clipping
four of the King's Guineas. Do you see that man here?

BROADBENT nods.

Can you point him out for me?

BROADBENT points at DAVID.

Did you witness that, Mr Parker?

PARKER

I did.

DIGHTON

See this man safely home.

PARKER and BROADBENT exit quickly through the main door, leaving DIGHTON to face the mob alone.

Some of the coiners start to approach DIGHTON, but DAVID gestures them back.
DAVID approaches DIGHTON and takes up a defiant stance, resulting in a face-off.

DAVID

Get out of here, taxman. Run like a chicken while you still can.

DIGHTON

Or what? You'll give me a thrashing like you thrash all the innocent folk who won't bow to your wretched ways?

DAVID

Either you are stupid coming in here talking big or you must think I'm witless, not knowing that you have men waiting outside to arrest me.

DIGHTON

No men. No bailiffs. Just me, and I will take you down.

DAVID

You're no match for me taxman. Stick to your books and balances or you'll leave here wishing you had. Get out now before they have to carry you out.

DAVID prepares to fight. In response, DIGHTON begins to circle, so that before his opponent realises it, DAVID is the closest to the door. At this point the BAILIFFS rush in and seize DAVID and set him in chains

You lying, cheating bastard! No bailiffs you said!

DIGHTON

I know your kind, Mr David Hartley. And I will do whatever it takes to put you where you belong. Get him off to gaol!

The BAILIFFS bustle DAVID out.

Before following them, DIGHTON addresses the coiners.

Let that be a lesson to you all. No more clipping and coining or I will take the lot of you down. The whole miserable pack of you will end up in gaol or worse.

Exit.

A moment's stunned silence among the coiners. Then ISAAC stands up as if to address them, but can't find the words.

COINER 1

(To ISAAC)

So what do we do now?'

Curtain.

ACT IV

(1769)

SCENE 1

Four days after the end of Act III.

York Gaol.

> *Grace, still pregnant, is visiting DAVID.*

DAVID

Did you bring food?

GRACE

(Gives him food)

Here. This'll do you good. And I've arranged for more to be brought.

DAVID

Good lass.

(Indicating her bump)

Everything all right?

GRACE

It's a gentle one, this. So far.

DAVID

You shouldn't have come all this way like that.

GRACE

I wanted to see you. We both wanted to be near you. I would have brought little David, too, and Mary, if I could, but they're too

111

young for such a journey. Bessy is looking after them. She's got her hands full, already, I know, but I'd do the same for her. We women have to help one another, otherwise I think the world would just stop.

DAVID

Did you pay the guard?

GRACE

There'll be no trouble from him. He knows where his bread's buttered.

DAVID

Need to keep sods like that happy. Get them onside.

GRACE

Ha! His eyes lit up when he saw gold. He'll leave us alone for a while.

DAVID

Good. We need to talk, private-like. There's things that need to be said.

GRACE

We have to get you out of here, that's the main thing. What can be done?

DAVID

They've got nowt on me except the word of a disloyal piece of scum. They're not charging me with forging Portuguese coins but with clipping the guineas, and that's a hanging offence. But without Broadbent's statement, they've got bugger all. Can't keep a man locked up without proof. Look at what happened to that man Greenwood. They arrested him on Broadbent's say-so, but had to let him out because the evidence came from a paid informant who was known to be a scoundrel and a liar in the first place. So we've got to get that lying scumbag Broadbent to retract his statement. All the miserable cur has to do is go to the magistrate and say that he was mistaken or that he was forced into giving evidence and he'll retract it in court, if he has to. Then it'll all just go away. You mark my words.

GRACE

He won't have the guts. He's afraid of you.

DAVID

Tell him I'll forgive him if he does as I say. Tell him I know he's an honest man and that they corrupted him with gold.

GRACE laughs.

GRACE

An honest man?

DAVID laughs too. They share the joke.

DAVID

Just tell him that. If he comes here, he'll receive my forgiveness. He'll believe you because he's as thick as the hide on a prize bull, but also because he knows what will happen if he doesn't.

GRACE

And if he still refuses? If he doesn't retract?

DAVID

He will. He just needs to be told. Told properly. And we've got loyal men that will tell him, if you know what I mean. The traitor might have taken the London King's guinea, but he can't hide and he can't run. We know where he lives. And if he ain't at home, his old man will be. Wouldn't want anything to happen to his old man, now would we? Nice old fellah! Would be such a shame. So do as I say. Get word to old man Broadbent that his son needs to sit down and have a bit of a think. A rethink, you might say. Will you do that, Grace?

GRACE

I'll do whatever it takes, David. Whatever it takes.

SCENE 2

Bell House. The following week.

The door to the yard is open. There is no sign of a furnace. Farmyard noises can be heard, especially chickens and a pig. GRACE, no longer pregnant, can be seen in the doorway feeding the animals. From within the house, her new baby cries.

GRACE

Oh, for God's sake, give me a minute's peace!

GRACE enters the house, leaving the door open; the farmyard noises continue. Seeing WILLIAM'S Bible, GRACE crosses herself.

Forgive me, Lord, for taking your name in vain, but sometimes I just need it all to stop!

I need the thoughts to stop. The thoughts that thrust themselves into my mind and tell me that the gold that descended on us as a blessing is in truth a curse, a glistering curse that poisons men's minds and makes them mad. Sometimes I think we are all mad; we each have our own private madness, but this lustrous mania has seized control of the valley. It drives men to shun their wives and neglect their farms and their children; they cut their fingers on the clipping scissors and burn their hands on the forge, but the frenzied flow of the molten mass of gold warps their minds and feeds their greed.

Out savage thoughts! Such weakness has no place in our world. The new way is the only way; it is our way now. And as the mantle passes to me, I must be strong. For David. For us all. I must be strong.

The baby cries become, louder. GRACE puts her hands to her ears.

Stop it! I can't take any more!

The farmyard noises become louder. GRACE collapses onto a chair, head in hands. The noises continue for a moment, then she sits up straight and utters a piercing scream.

Blackout.

SCENE 3

Scene: the same.

*When the lights go up, the rear door is closed and GRACE is
seated in the same place, cradling/feeding a baby. All is quiet.
GRACE is perfectly calm.*

GRACE

There, my sweet. My, my, you were hungry weren't you? We were
all hungry, weren't we? Man, woman, child and beast, all need
feeding. Did I say man? We haven't got a man now, well just your
uncle Isaac, I suppose, but he's off doing what it is that they do and
that we don't talk about. And his bible-bashing old man is off to
chapel, so it's just us now to enjoy the peace and quiet. There were
noises, but they've gone, now. Sometimes I just can't stand it.
Sometimes I just can't stand anything. And sometimes it just all
stops. Sometimes I just sit here and I can't move, can't lift my arms.
And I can see, but I can't see; it's just like I'm there but I'm not
there. I can feel my heart beating, but it's so heavy, so heavy. And
nothing makes any sense, and nothing matters. Nothing matters and
yet everything matters. It's like God has moved out, taken his
blessing away, so that everything is just a burden. I could die and I
wouldn't care. The house could catch fire and I wouldn't even
notice.

Baby gurgles. She wipes its face.

But there I go again, talking my head off. One day you'll
understand. Maybe. Anyway, your mummy's all right now. It's just
one of those things that comes and goes, like rain and sunshine.
Sometimes it's one and sometimes the other. Ups and downs. Hills
and dales. But it's our secret. When there's other folk around, I try
to keep going even in the bad times, but it's so hard, so hard… I

117

feel my soul trapped in a swinging gate that is neither open nor shut, but at times it's like an elemental force that makes me stronger, and I've got to be strong now, haven't I, my sweet? Haven't I?

A knock at the door.

Who's that?

BROADBENT enters. GRACE lays the baby in a cot.

BROADBENT

It's me, missus. They said as likes you want to see me. They say you sent word.

GRACE

You're a thieving, lying parasite, James Broadbent, but aye, I sent word. And I think you know why.

BROADBENT

No, missus, I don't know as what I can do for you now that...

GRACE

...now that what? Say it!

BROADBENT

...now that King David ain't here no more. Ain't nobody to give me orders any more, except yon Duke of York, yon Isaac, an' he ain't here, is he, cause he's down at Barbary's, where I would be if...

GRACE

... where you would be if you weren't afraid to show your miserable face, you mean? I've got your measure, James Broadbent, and I know what you did. I know who you are, James Broadbent. Do you know who I am?

BROADBENT

I know who you are, missus, you are King David's missus, missus.

GRACE

Hold your tongue, you malevolent scourge of the earth! I am not my husband's chattel! I am a force you have awakened with your treachery, and if God doesn't strike you down, I will! You have betrayed your King.

BROADBENT

Pardon me, missus, but you are a woman, and King David's business is man's business.

GRACE

You are no man, you are a snivelling coward, and I am your worst enemy. One word from me, and you will be torn limb from limb. I am not my husband, nor his servant, but I am his vengeance. If you do not fear God's wrath, you had surely better fear mine!

BROADBENT

I came because I was sent for, missus, and I have heard what you have to say, and now I will take my leave.

(He heads for the door.)

GRACE

Stay!

BROADBENT stops, turns.

BROADBENT

I know what you think of me, missus, and maybe it's true that you can give orders, and maybe it's true that there's others that wish me harm and may think to waylay me, but that's as it may be. I knows what's what, and I'll take my chances. So it's good day to you, missus.

119

GRACE

No, you haven't yet heard what I have to say. You haven't heard what you are going to do.

BROADBENT

Oh? And what am I going to do?

GRACE

(Calmly)

You are going to go back to the magistrate in Bradford and you are going to tell him that you were mistaken, that you never saw anybody in this house or from this house clipping or coining or helping to clip or coin or heard anybody in this family ever talk of the clipping or coining, that you were told to say these things by that exciseman Dighton, and that you are sorry, but you now realise your mistake.

BROADBENT

(Laughing)

And why should I do that, and what makes you think you can order me around?

GRACE

(Very slowly and clearly)

Because you love your father.

BROADBENT

(Stunned)

What?

GRACE

Your father is very dear to you; a kind old man who may not have long to enjoy God's favour on this earth.

BROADBENT

Hah! He's as fit as a fiddle!

GRACE

(Very slowly)

That's as may be, but you never know what's around the corner. Or who.

BROADBENT

You wouldn't do that. Order them to harm an innocent old man.

GRACE

An old man who begat a villain and a traitor.

BROADBENT

You can't do that.

GRACE

You have just admitted that I can. I rule Bell House now and I can order whatever I like.

BROADBENT

But I can't go back to the magistrate. He'll never believe me. And if he does, they will set King David free, and then he will come after me. I won't do it.

GRACE

First you will go to York and beg my husband's forgiveness, which he will grant you. Then you will make a statement that you were mistaken or that you were unfairly placed under pressure to make false accusations against my husband, that you retract everything. Do you understand?

BROADBENT

And King David will forgive me?

GRACE

You have my word. Do you understand?

BROADBENT

Yes, I understand.

GRACE

So you will do the right thing. And do you understand what will happen if you don't do the right thing?

BROADBENT

Yes, I understand.

GRACE

And do you agree?

BROADBENT

Yes, I agree.

GRACE

Tomorrow, then. Waste no time. Now leave!

Exit BROADBENT. GRACE picks up the baby.

There, my little darling. Mummy has done what had to be done. Sometimes you just have to be strong. I don't know if God is watching us, or if even if there is a God, but sometimes you just have to do what you feel is right and then the world just falls into place, and the satisfaction warms your heart like the sweetest milk straight from the stove, sweeter than any honey, sweeter than love, sweeter even than life itself.

SCENE 4

York Gaol.

GRACE is visiting DAVID.

DAVID

(Loudly)

You're looking well, lass. How's everybody at home?

GRACE

We all miss you, especially the little ones, but we're bearing up. Baby Isaac looks just like you. I couldn't bring him, but you'll love him when you see him, when you get out. Bessy and Edie are looking after them all.

DAVID

(Whispering)

Is the guard taken care of?

GRACE

He's getting himself some ale. A guinea goes a long way with his sort.

DAVID

Good lass. That thing we talked about last time. The scumbag was here begging for forgiveness. Has he changed his statement?

GRACE

He's been to see that exciseman Dighton again, to explain that he was... er... mistaken. Well, anybody can make a mistake, now, can't they?

DAVID

(Laughs)

They can indeed. Honest mistake, that's all it was. All too easy to get confused, especially in the poor light. Especially when I wasn't even there. He probably wasn't even there either for that matter. Might have just dreamed it, who knows? Has he made a written statement? It has to be in writing and get to the court before the Spring Assizes, the sooner the better.

GRACE

He's going back see the magistrate in Bradford. He does all the writing down.

DAVID

And there's another thing that needs to be done. Not just for me, but for all of us.

(Looking around, then quietly)

The exciseman has to go. He's the one who turned our own against us. He's the one promising false gold in return for treachery. As long as he's still around, none of us are safe. He'll bribe others, he'll drive a wedge between us, ruin our business and attack our family. As sure as it rains in Cragg Vale, he'll come after us all. He'll come after Isaac. He'll come after William. He'll take the food out of our children's mouths, just as they were getting used to eating every day. We'll be back to eating nettles if he has his way. He has to go, Grace. He'll be the ruin of us all if he isn't stopped.

GRACE

Tell me what to do.

DAVID

Speak to our Isaac.

GRACE

He won't like it. He doesn't want to make things worse. He thinks we have to wait till it all blows over.

DAVID

Make things worse? How could they be worse? I'm still King of the Valley and you can tell that brother of mine that what I say goes! Unless it's my place that he wants to step into. Is that it?

GRACE

No-one could ever take your place, David. Not in the Valley. Not in my heart. You know that.

DAVID

All I'm saying is, you know what needs to be done. I don't care how it's done, as long as it's done. Promise me, Grace. Promise me that you'll make it happen.

GRACE

I'm only a woman, David, but I'll do whatever I can.

DAVID

Do whatever it takes.

GRACE

Yes, David. I promise: I'll do whatever it takes.

(To herself)

Whatever it takes.

SCENE 5

Bell House.

*GRACE is doing household chores. ISAAC enters from the
yard. GRACE stops what she is doing and confronts him.*

GRACE

You've got to do something.

ISAAC

Like what? David locked up in York Castle. He's already due for
trial. We'll never get him out of there. Broadbent has changed his
tune, but they're not listening.

GRACE

You never used to be such a lily-livered lump of a lout. Either get
David out or at least stop them coming for the rest of us.

ISAAC

It's that Dighton. He's got it in for us. We'll have to put things on
hold for a while. No more clipping till it's all blown over.

GRACE

This is our way of life now. I can't go back to the old days. I'm not
going to let the babbies starve. It'll never blow over unless you do
something.

ISAAC

There's nothing to be done unless we can get Dighton out of the
way.

GRACE

There you go, then.

ISAAC

Too dangerous! He's a tax inspector, for God's sake! Anyway, I can't. They'll know, and then they'll come straight for me.

GRACE

There are others.

ISAAC

Others?

GRACE

Them with an eye for an unclipped guinea, them as got more brawn than brains.

ISAAC

How?

GRACE

You used to be a gunsmith.

Beat.

ISAAC

No. Any sign of a firearm and I'm the first person they'd suspect. And even if I'm overheard asking around...

GRACE

You don't even have to do that; just get whatever you need and have a quiet word with Thomas Clayton. He can be trusted. He can find someone. A couple of heavies from Hepton or Sowerby. Promise them a hundred guineas from the box.

ISAAC

No.

GRACE

Do it for me. You once said you'd do anything for me.

ISAAC

That was… that was… before.

GRACE

That's it then! It's all over. King David, our golden years, you, me. All finished. Get out and don't come back!

ISAAC heads to the door, stops, turns.

ISAAC

It's murder you're talking about. You know that?

GRACE

It's what they've done to us, they murdered the poor, murdered our land, took away our livelihood and murdered our babbies. Eighteen hours at the loom and living on oatmeal porridge. It was murder when they sent our menfolk off to war, it was murder when there was no doctor there for your old mum, and it's murder us all they will, if we can't carry on clipping and coining. And now they want to hang my dearest David; they want to murder your brother – and for what? For looking after his own when no one else would or could. If taking our king from us isn't murder, I don't know what is. And it's up to you now; you're his rightful heir. That's why they call you the Duke of York. It's your duty to take over, to take charge, to earn the respect that's due to you. Make folks look up to you the way they looked up to him; make folks follow you, make people…

(Sotto voce)

…love you. Dighton is nothing to us. Worse than nothing. He's a monster out to destroy us. It's no sacrifice at all. It's just one human life to protect the hundreds of good, honest folk that will suffer if the beast and his cronies have their way. You're not doing anything to them that they haven't already done to us. It's for David. For you. For me.

> *(Beat.)*

For us. And to tell the truth, it isn't murder. It's retribution. It's justice.

ISAAC

Edie!

> *Enter Edie*

Go find Thomas Clayton. Tell him I need to see him. Tonight at Barbary's.

EDIE

Yes, Master!

> *Exit EDIE.*

GRACE

You see. You're coming into your own at last.

ISAAC

What do you mean?

GRACE

Even Edie knows you're the master now.

SCENE 6

Spotlight on ELLA

ELLA

When they write the history books, they'll tell you of the great men of Halifax, of bankers and merchants and engineers, of clergymen, lawyers and others of the black cloth. But you won't read about the men who kept them all in check, who made sure they kept orderly ledgers and paid their dues. And they won't tell you about the women behind the men who kept them in check. Look at me. Eight children I've borne to my dear William, and time and time again we have been uprooted and made to travel the country, forced to make a new home for ourselves in unfamiliar surroundings, thrust into the midst of strange-sounding folk, the like of which we don't know and sometimes can't fathom. Coming here was hard, and settling down is even harder when you don't know how long your stay is to last. To be fair, we've been here nigh on ten years now and have set up a nice home in Bull Green, right in the middle of town, but with William's work, we never know when the call will come to move on. Here in this county, he is loved by some and loathed by others. Those that would abuse him call him 'tax collector', but he is much more than that; he is charged by the King's authority with the responsibility not only of securing the revenues but of investigating false reporting and uncovering misdeeds.

His is an honest profession and he commands the respect of the merchants and traders he calls on, but he is a man, too, and needs the welcoming hearth of home, needs to spend time with his wife and children, and it is we who are often dealt the short hand by his long hours of work and duties beyond the normal calling.

Oftentimes I fear for him when he is out and about his business, sometimes in the daylight mass of heaving humanity in the town, sometimes at night in dark alleys and sometimes striding alone across the vast moor to far-flung inns and homesteads populated by hostile publicans, millers, farmers and the like. Such is no company for me, nor am I at peace among the pressures of town society and although I could yearn for more courage, I rarely venture out but wait with a thundering heart for my William to come home. This is not a bright place, but some days are darker than others and on the darkest days, his absence seems to bring all the wind and rain of Yorkshire whistling and howling through my windows as I pray for his safe return. That's my daily prayer, for my husband's safe return. His safe return. Nothing more.

SCENE 7

Bell House.

> *GRACE is going about her domestic chores.*
>
> *A dog barks. ISAAC enters.*

GRACE

Is it done?

ISAAC

I've set it in motion. That's all you need to know.

GRACE

When?

ISAAC

You don't need to know that.

> *Pause.*

Dighton's away, but he'll be back. Soon.

GRACE

I wish things were different.

ISAAC

I know.

GRACE

Things could have been different.

ISAAC

A lot of things could have been different. A long time ago.

GRACE

But this is what we have now.

ISAAC

Yes.

ISAAC looks around.

GRACE

They've all gone to the market.

GRACE goes into the bedroom. After a moment, ISAAC follows.

SCENE 8

Street outside Dighton's House near Bull Green, Halifax. Night.

This scene may be acted out in full view of the audience or partly offstage / behind a wall or hedge, but however it is staged, no attempt must be made to hide the sheer brutality involved. The actions are horrific, and this must be evident in the performance.

NORMINGTON, THOMAS and CLAYTON are in hiding, waiting for DIGHTON to return home.

NORMINGTON

(Whispering)

Are you sure he'll be back tonight?

CLAYTON

He will. Trust me.

NORMINGTON

Hah! You said that last time. That's three nights we've spent waiting for the lousy taxman to show up. I can't face another night standing around here freezing – and we can't risk being seen.

THOMAS

(Brandishing the gun)

And I can't keep carrying this thing around with me everywhere I go. If we don't get him tonight…

CLAYTON

Shhhh! Someone's coming.

A figure approaches. NORMINGTON raises his pistol, but is restrained by CLAYTON. The figure passes by and exits.

134

That's not him. He's bigger than that – and he'll be dressed up all fine and dandy.

NORMINGTON

Not short of a few guineas for a fine pair of breeches, his type. But you know what King David said: it's our turn now. We've a right to…

CLAYTON

Shut up. You've got a job to do, that's all. You've been paid to get it done and keep your mouth shut, and that's all there is to it. Shhh!

Enter DIGHTON.

NORMINGTON

Is that him?

CLAYTON

That's him. Like I say, he's a big bugger, but he's no match for you two now.

DIGHTON approaches the house. NORMINGTON and THOMAS hesitate.

THOMAS

You sure that's him?

CLAYTON

That's him. Go to it…. Now!

As THOMAS and NORMINGTON break cover, CLAYTON hurries off, leaving them alone with DIGHTON.

DIGHTON hears them, turns. At that moment NORMINGTON fires, shooting him in the head. DIGHTON falls.

THOMAS

You got him!

Pause.

Is he dead?

DIGHTON stirs.

THOMAS fires at the body on the ground. DIGHTON is still moving.

NORMINGTON

He will be when I've finished with him.

THOMAS stands transfixed as NORMINGTON begins to stamp on DIGHTON'S body. Then THOMAS, too, joins in. When they are satisfied with their efforts, they stand and look down at the body.

THOMAS

Let's see what he's got on him. Must have some gold about him, or a watch, or something.

They bend down to rob the body, holding up and inspecting each stolen item.

NORMINGTON

That's all he's got, but it'll do.

ELLA

(From the doorway)

What's going on? Who's there?

THOMAS

Let's get out of here!

ELLA comes out of the house, accompanied by MARY.

ELLA sees DIGHTON'S body, rushes to him and lets out a bloodcurdling scream.

Curtain.

ACT V
(1769-1770)

SCENE 1

November 1769.

Spotlight on Ella. She is in mourning.

ELLA

Today I buried my husband, watched his body sink beneath the earth of this godforsaken corner of a crushing world. I never thought I was capable of hate, but I hate this place, this horrible, evil-smelling cesspit of a mudhole in this barren, devil-infested county full of criminals and cut-throats who think nothing about shooting an honest family man in the head, then stamping him to death and robbing his corpse. Robbing me of my husband and our children of their father. And robbing William of the chance to watch them grow up and take their place in the world, robbing him of his mature years.

Eight children I've borne to my William and four of them still at home, for me to bring up on my own. How am I going to feed them now? How am I going to pay for their upkeep and schooling? If it weren't for Ann and Robert Parker, I'd be penniless and destitute by now. Robert persuaded Lord Rockingham to write to the Treasury and ask them to grant me a pension in recognition of what my William did to rid this town of the yellow rabble. But they need a father! A father! Not more gold! It's the gold that's done for us all! The gold, the gold, that's all you hear in this town. Clip and coin. Gold and yellow. Rob and kill. It's not revenge I want, but justice.

It has taken this to drag me forth from the confines of my four walls, to release me from my inner prison and set me free to wreak the havoc of wrath that those puny spirits of hell are too stunted to perceive. I will storm across any battlefield, soar over any armies, to see the arrows of retribution rain down on the villains and their treacherous kin.

If I were a man, I'd stamp the murdering bastards to death myself. As a woman, the hurricane of my anger is no less brutal, and I will find a way to ravage their souls and tear out their hearts as they have torn mine from my breast. Beware, you heathen hordes. I will come for you!

SCENE 2

Bell House.

BESSY and GRACE are busy with household chores.

BESSY

(At the window)

There's someone coming.

GRACE

(Joining BESSY at the window)

Not one of ours in her smart city frocks and silken town bonnet.

BESSY

And she's not behaving like one of us, either. Leaping and twirling like a four-year old. Going to break an ankle, like as not. Shall I chase her away?

GRACE

(Looking round the room)

No, we've nothing to fear now. Let her come.

BESSY opens the door. A few moments later, ELLA enters at a rush, prancing over the threshold.

ELLA

I came across the moor, across the open barren landscape of mud and slime, scrub and bracken, thorn and nettle, and yet it is not the squish and crinkle underfoot that drove me on, but the vastness of the sky, the distant haze of far horizons that at first so engulfed my eyesight that my vision was overwhelmed, my breath so stifled in my chest and my heart pounded like a blacksmith's hammer, for never these ten years have I seen such a sight, hidden away as I

140

was for fear of the world, for fear of the expanse of uncluttered space, that I have rarely ventured out of my home and then only to adhere to the walls of the tallest edifices as I groped my way through the narrow streets. But now, driven by my fury and incensed by the gross injustice you and your kind have unleashed, I raced across this barren heath, headlong to this your miserable dwelling, from where you and yours have unleashed such a horror that was unimaginably greater than the terror I felt at exposing myself to this tortuous vastness. And yet, and yet, as I lurched and stumbled across this harsh terrain, whipped ever forwards by the fierce winds of wrath, I felt myself return to childhood, fancied myself flying fleet of foot over the rich soil and green grass of the giddy girlish delight of long distant days, drinking in the free, heavenly air of sweet forgotten infancy.

BESSY

Have a care, Grace. She has lunacy in her eyes.

BESSY backs away from ELLA, but GRACE stands her ground.

GRACE

(To ELLA)

I don't know who you are, but I think you are mad indeed.

ELLA

(Ignoring her)

The grey, sloping hillsides, the cloudlike sheep and sheep-like clouds sent my soul spiralling out of control, arms out, circling round and round and yet pressing ever forward, toward the goal of this infernal place, perceiving this pestilent pit of your sinful sordidness, this, your damned hole of a hovel, growing from a bruise on the landscape to a pile of stones formed into a gateway of hell where you and your criminal cronies brandish the fire of Satan to gild his favour and spew out his spawn to corrupt, maim and kill, to slaughter the innocent, to strike down the pure of heart and stamp them to death beneath your filthy feet...

GRACE

I know now who you are.

ELLA

You cannot know the torment it took to tame my trepidation and yet you too will tremble with terror and your agony will surpass my anguish before I have done with you. I see you now before me, crouched in your den of vipers from which you will never emerge, for I will make you regret every evil you have ever done.

GRACE

You know nothing of me.

ELLA

I know what you are. You are a vile corruption of womanhood, a wanton wench who could not keep her husband from villainy and depravity. If there were any justice in this world, both you and your lying, cheating husband would swing from a rope.

GRACE

My husband has never cheated, but maybe you are right; maybe I am not without guilt, but what of it? Who are you to judge me? Who are you to think you know me?

ELLA looks at GRACE, then at BESSY, then back to GRACE.

ELLA

I know.

GRACE

How can you know? What do you know?

Beat.

ELLA

I know... I know you are Queen to the bastard who calls himself King, the clipper and coiner and craven coward whose word rules the criminal curs of this godforsaken valley.

GRACE

I am no queen and never meant to be, and never will be. I seek only to feed my children. In this, I think we are sisters.

ELLA

Sisters! Never!

ELLA hurls herself at GRACE; they tussle. BESSY tries to separate them but can't. Then GRACE suddenly gives in and allows ELLA to strike her. GRACE falls to the ground.

Blackout.

SCENE 3

Later the same day.

The lights come up on GRACE and BESSY. ELLA has left.

BESSY

She's no match for you. Why didn't you defend yourself?

GRACE

The best defence is not always through force; violence is the man's way: 'Hit me and I hit you' is the man's answer to everything. But my defence is a much better one; I know who is the stronger, I have no need to prove it. Should I tear her hair out and scratch her eyeballs to blood simply to prove my pride of place? For what? I have a much better victory in my heart by knowing I am the force she is not.

And I have defended our stronghold for all of us. She has her satisfaction and will not pursue us through the courts. It is over.

BESSY

I don't think it will ever be over. I feel a heaviness in the air that carries beyond the Valley.

GRACE

All the same, she has her satisfaction and I have my husband.

BESSY

For now.

GRACE

Don't say that!

(Beat.)

But I think you're right.

144

BESSY

About what?

GRACE

That it will never be over. They say it will never be over if it's true.

BESSY

What?

GRACE

Love. That's why we have to be strong.

BESSY

You've lost me.

GRACE

I can't go on, Bessy.

BESSY

You're strong, Grace. You will always get through. And even if we go back to the old ways, we have had good times we wouldn't have had without the gold.

GRACE is now sitting with her arms by her side, staring ahead as if paralysed, trance-like. She speaks in a monotone.

GRACE

It's not that. It's the other thing that's dragging me down.

BESSY

What?

GRACE

She's right. That excise woman has a gift. She knows. Of all the bigwigs and gentry and lawyers and lawmen and those who would

145

tread us down and seek to put an end to our living, she is the only one who knows.

BESSY

Knows what?

GRACE

She knows my guilt. She could sense it.

BESSY

Your guilt? But you've done nothing. All you ever did was feed the babies, tend the fields and pluck the chickens.

GRACE

I plucked more than a chicken. I plucked the heart out of her husband. It was me, Bessy. I set Isaac onto the deed.

BESSY

Isaac? My Isaac? What has my Isaac got to do with it?

GRACE

Nothing.

BESSY

You said it. You can't unsay it. What do you mean, Grace?

(Shouting)

Are you going to drag him down, too? Is my Isaac going to disappear in the night, be manhandled out of Barbary's in the sight of all? Grace, what have you done?

GRACE

Nothing. Everything.

Pause. GRACE gradually recovers from her trance-like state.

Bessy, I don't know what's next, but you can't be seen here any longer. Or at home. You have to move on. Isaac has skills; he can find work. Or get yourself a farm, away from the gold and the temptation; you can take half the sheep, half the chickens; you'll be safe there. They won't come for me if there are no menfolk here, and they won't come for Isaac if he's away from the coining.

BESSY

Isaac will decide what we do.

GRACE

(Firmly)

No. I decide now. Tell Isaac I…

BESSY

Tell him what?

GRACE

Tell him… Tell him to bring the cart and collect his things. I won't be here when he comes. I don't want to see him any more.

BESSY

Why not?

GRACE

Don't ask.

BESSY

What are you saying?

GRACE

I did it for David. I promised to do… whatever it takes.

BESSY

My Isaac…? You hussy! You whore…. You….

(Flies at her, screaming and flailing.)

Blackout.

SCENE 4

A Street.

BESSY is leaning against a wall, waiting. ANN enters. She is on her way home.

BESSY

Excuse me, madam.

ANN

Yes, what is it.

BESSY

It's Mrs Parker, isn't it? Wife of the lawyer, Robert Parker.

ANN

What of it?

BESSY

There is something you need to know.

ANN

This is no place to talk.

BESSY

It will have to do. I won't be seen in any fancy places with a lady like you, and you won't want to be seen with the likes of me, I guess.

ANN

Say what you have to say, then leave me be.

BESSY

Gladly, my lady. I have a message for your husband.

ANN

A message? From whom?

BESSY

Doesn't matter 'from whom'. It's about the man they call King David.

ANN

What about him? He's in York Castle. He's going to hang.

BESSY

No, he will be set free. The evidence they have against him for the coining won't hold. All they have is the word of a proven liar; others charged on similar evidence have already been freed. His family have already received word.

ANN

So? What has that got to do with me? What do you want?

BESSY

I want justice, nothing more. An eye for an eye, a heart for a heart.

ANN

Stop talking in riddles woman. Say what you have to say, then go.

BESSY

Just this. They will let David Hartley out unless they have a reason not to.

ANN

What reason?

BESSY

Your husband's friend, the exciseman. Something happened to him.

ANN

Everybody knows that. But Hartley was already in gaol.

BESSY

He had a visitor.

ANN

What are you saying?

BESSY

A visitor who passed on his instructions.

ANN

You?

BESSY

No, not me. And it doesn't matter who. I'm just telling you that the plan to deal with the taxman came from the top, from King David himself.

ANN

Can you prove it?

BESSY

I don't need to prove it. I'm not a fancy lawyer or a fancy lawyer's wife. I'm just giving you some information. That's what people have been doing, isn't it? Giving you information.

ANN

And I suppose you want paying? For that?

BESSY

I want nothing from you.

ANN

Nothing?

BESSY

From you, nothing. From a hooded man in York, the sweet taste of justice. They say you can't heal the hurt of a broken heart, but you can spread the agony around and hope to dilute it. A word can break a heart and a rope can snap a neck in return.

ANN

You are not the only one to want that.

BESSY

I know. Your lawyer-husband wants the same, but it will take a woman's wiles to incite him to action.

ANN

How on earth do I do that?

BESSY

You will find a way.

ANN

And how can he do what you say and stay within the law?

BESSY

He will find a way. He is a lawyer. The law will say what he wants it to say, and when well-spoken to, a judge will do what he wants him to do.

ANN

I've never heard such nonsense!

BESSY

I know. Because we never had this little chat. And we never met.

ANN

That's right. We never met.

BESSY

Remember that; and remember all the other details. And tell your husband to make sure the exciseman's widow is looked after. She has suffered enough. We have all suffered from this yellow scourge and it must end.

ANN

Thank you for your concern. My husband has already obtained a pension for Mrs Dighton.

(Beat.)

Do you know, I am beginning to wish we had met.

BESSY

We never met.

Exit.

ANN

No, we never met.

Exit.

SCENE 5

An inn.

ROCKINGHAM is seated at a table, reading a letter. Wine has been served.

PARKER enters.

PARKER

You wanted to see me, my lord?

ROCKINGHAM

Indeed, Mr Parker. I have some news. Some very good news indeed.

(Indicating the letter)

I have finally received a reply from the government in London, from the Lord of the Treasury. Listen to this: 'I received last night the honour of Your Lordship's letter of the first instant, relative to the murder of Dighton, and the alarming practice of clipping and coining, which has got to so great a height; and having laid the same before the King, His Majesty was graciously pleased to approve the steps that have been taken and the zeal and activity which the gentlemen of the county have entered into in the matter.'

PARKER

So we have the King's approval, but does this really make a difference?

ROCKINGHAM

There's more. It seems, my dear Parker, that Lord Weymouth, our esteemed Lord of the Treasury, fond as he is of gambling and quaffing, has finally and got off his fat arse and urged the

153

government to support our efforts at the public expense; his exact words, 'at the public expense'.

PARKER

That means that they have finally woken up and taken notice. Horrifying to think that it has taken a gang of thieves and counterfeiters to put Yorkshire on their map. For all their talk of a level bowling green throughout England, indeed the whole of Britain, this is the first time that we can expect actual help.

ROCKINGHAM

When I was prime minister, it was always my ambition to release the economic power of this great county. I was cast out of favour before I could set such great things in motion, but at least in this, we have the upper hand. And yet, it is nothing other than a triumph of common reason.

PARKER

Ha! Because their coffers have suffered.

ROCKINGHAM

Indeed. Nevertheless, we are now asked to: Quote 'take such measures as may be judged proper in order to put an end to this criminal practice of coining and clipping in the West Riding of Yorkshire.' Unquote. And they are sending Mr Chamberlayne the Solicitor of the Mint, to Halifax, together with men and means, to help us secure convictions. It's no holds-barred from now on, Mr Parker.

PARKER

But what about that felon, David Hartley? If he is released, it will only fire up the clippers and coiners to persist and resist, or cower and hide where we can least surprise them.

ROCKINGHAM

Surely he is going to hang after the Spring Assizes?

PARKER

That is far from certain. We still have the rule of law in this country, and the magistrates in York base their judgements and sentences on admissible evidence, not on the vileness of character of the accused.

ROCKINGHAM

But Hartley stands accused by the evidence of a first-hand account. A reliable witness.

PARKER

A witness, certainly, but a proven rogue, a treacherous fiend and paid informer by the name of Broadbent. And he has retracted his statement.

ROCKINGHAM

Do you have that in writing?

PARKER

I have a letter to that effect from Mr Leedes, the magistrate in Bradford, who took down his original statement. And Broadbent is prepared to go to York and retract his statement there if need be. At the last Assizes in York, all but one of the coiners facing conviction and hanging were released on bail or reprieved. The York magistrates will not convict without good purpose.

ROCKINGHAM

So unless we have something else against Hartley, he will go free.

PARKER

We are not above the law, My Lord.

ROCKINGHAM

And yet as Lord Lieutenant of our great county, I am not without influence. Find me some leverage, Mr Parker. A legal or moral reason to press our case with the trial magistrate in York.

Enter ANN. She and PARKER hold a whispered conversation.

PARKER

My Lord, I have it on good authority that David Hartley ordered the killing of Superintendent Dighton.

ROCKINGHAM

Well, now, if that doesn't sway our case in York, I don't know what will. The magistrate may be lenient when it comes to counterfeiting, but a whiff of murder is another matter entirely. I will write to York immediately. And it will suffice to seal the matter if Broadbent's retraction is not heard in time to prevent a sentence being carried out.

PARKER

I will be indebted to you, my lord. William Dighton was my friend and I will rejoice to see justice done.

ROCKINGHAM

(Raising his glass)

To justice!

PARKER

To justice!

Blackout.

SCENE 6

Spotlight on GRACE.

GRACE

There is no justice. I know that. I have always known that. Or there are many kinds of justice. There's one justice for the farmer and weaver, whose lot it is to always remain poor, for the hardy men and women who scrape a living in the harsh climes of Cragg Vale and Erringden Moor, for the downtrodden folk of our Valley of Gold where the glowing corn makes your heart sing in summer and the piercing wind tears holes in your skin in winter.

And there is another justice for the lords and ladies dressed in fine silks and satins with their pigskin gloves and lambswool raiments who cling to their opulence in fields of lavender and clover, for the far-off despots and dictators, the bullies and barons of the distant capital who cavort and skulk in their castles and palaces and who only ever came to Yorkshire to quash us.

And yet I believe in justice; call it my lunacy, if you fancy to do so, but the blood in my veins tells me there is a deeper justice, an inner truth that we all share, a faith that in some unfathomable way, we all know what is right and what is wrong and we rise and fall by that deeper sense of justice, the justice of the heart.

SCENE 7

Outside the courtroom in York Castle. April 1770.

Grace is sitting on a bench and waiting. After a moment or two, ISAAC enters.

GRACE

Is there any word?

ISAAC

They have reprieved almost all the men charged with counterfeiting. They are to be given bail until the autumn Assizes. That's over a dozen death sentences quashed already.

GRACE

What about David?

ISAAC

Nothing yet. They will let us know as soon as there is.

GRACE

It is too late.

DAVID

It is not too late. David's sentence has already been questioned. Broadbent is waiting to see the magistrate. Men are often reprieved at the last minute.

GRACE

They have already prepared the gallows at Tyburn.

Enter MESSENGER

What news?

MESSENGER

More men have been freed. Only three sentences still stand.

ISAAC

Who? Their names, man!

MESSENGER

James Oldfield, William Varley and David Hartley, but the magistrate is still deliberating. There is talk of a reprieve.

Exit.

ISAAC

Did you hear that? A reprieve.

GRACE

They will show no mercy. They are afraid of him.

Re-enter MESSENGER.

MESSENGER

One man has been reprieved.

ISAAC

Who? The name, the name!

MESSENGER

William Varley has been set free. David Hartley's case is to be referred to the High Sheriff.

Exit.

DAVID

There is still hope.

GRACE

There may be hope, but there is no time.

ISAAC

We can only wait.

GRACE

You should not be here.

ISAAC

I will not let you face this alone.

GRACE

This is my torment, mine only. There is nothing you can do except save yourself. You must flee.

ISAAC

Any danger I face here is nothing to what you must bear. And if David must face his fate, you still have me.

GRACE

You?

ISAAC

You know that there is a bond between us. Whatever happens, there will always be life. There will always be love.

GRACE

That is what you do not understand. You were there for me, I know that, but I love David. I love my husband. Oh, it's not the love of instant passion, but the love that grows with time. Not what we might have had, you and I, if things had been different, not something born of instant attraction and desire, but a much stronger force, a love that is born of flimsy duty and becomes more solid, more permanent in the heart, a longing and a belonging that sits deeper and at times hangs heavy and at other times unfolds its wings like a dove and conjures sunshine from the darkness.

160

ISAAC

I will wait with you. Forever, if need be.

GRACE

There is no hope. Go.

ISAAC

There is always hope.

GRACE

There was never hope. I have ordered a coffin.

ISAAC

It can't end this way.

GRACE

Leave me.

ISAAC

I can't. Not now.

GRACE

Go back to Bessy.

Pause.

If you won't go, I will.

Exit. ISAAC remains until the scene changes.

SCENE 8

York Tyburn at Knavesmire.

A crowd of citizens line the road to the gallows. ELLA is among them. Crowd noises. The hubbub grows.

CITIZEN 1

Is that him in the cart? They all look the same to me.

CITIZEN 2

Maybe it isn't him.

ELLA

That's him. Even from here, I can see the evil in his eyes. There's no mistake. I will not have travelled from Halifax in vain.

CITIZEN 2

You came all that way for this?

ELLA

I came to see it with my own eyes.

CITIZEN 2

Any minute now.

CITIZEN 1

They say he was a King.

CITIZEN 3

Some say he was just a common thug.

CITIZEN 1

They're all the same to yon Jack Ketch.

CITIZEN 3

Aye, the hangman don't care how mighty they think they are.

CITIZEN 1

The cart's in place.

CITIZEN 2

So's the rope.

CITIZEN 3

Here goes!

> *A cry goes up among the crowd, some voices cheering, some lamenting.*

CITIZEN 1

Look at him squirm and kick. This'll take a while.

CITIZEN 2

Horrible way to go.

CITIZEN 1

He's stopped struggling.

CITIZEN 2

It is done.

ELLA

A lesson for the rest of his kind.

GRACE

(Entering and speaking unseen)

We are all his kind.

> *The crowd parts, revealing GRACE as the speaker. She is holding a bunch of violets. She is accompanied by priest, followers and a coffin on a cart. A death knell tolls. The crowd falls silent.*

I come to claim my own.

> *Curtain.*

EPILOGUE
(1774)

Bell House. Autumn

Grace is packing her belongings.

GRACE

So there you have it. They hanged my darling David, and I
received special permission to bring his body back to the Valley,
this valley of his birth, this Valley of Gold. They lined the streets
from Halifax to Hebden to watch him pass and followed his
cortege all the way up the steep cobbles of The Buttress to the
church of St Thomas à Becket in Heptonstall, where we laid him to
rest in proper consecrated ground, a burial fit for the king he truly
was. And after my David was betrayed, the hangman was kept
busy until the powers from afar had stamped out our independence
and returned to their palace in Westminster. My David was
mourned throughout the Upper Calder Valley and his grave is kept
clean to this day.

Others it was who were hanged in chains on Beacon Hill, the
murderers Robert Thomas and Mathew Normington among them, a
reminder of our lawlessness, they said, but it wasn't that. It was a
reminder of what they did to level us down, to drag us to the pit of
their foreign, tax-hungry immorality. But they cannot prevent new
life from springing up here in this, our once happy valley. I gave
birth three times whilst they were bickering over filings and ounces,
and King David will live on through our children and their
children's children.

And as autumn follows summer and drags us, dogs, horse, cart and
all, into winter, you have to look forward, not back. They've got
machines now that will do the weaving of ten men, machines in the
field to end the backbreaking drudgery, and turnpikes and canals to

shift our grain and woollens faster than ever before. It's a grand new world of freedom and leisure we can look to. But not here in this mansion of memories where only the past lives on.

As for the present, there's no place for me here now that David's father has joined his dear Rosie in a better place. I'm moving to Lodge Farm as soon as I hand over the brass to yon tightwad Walker. Why do I say that? We're all tight-fisted here, except in the generosity of our hearts. All the same, he wants paying in gold, not brass; well, it's a good job I always put a bit aside before it was washed down the drain hole at Barbary's ale house.

There is a knock at the door.

Edie! See who that is.

Enter EDIE.

EDIE

It's Mr Walker, ma'am.

GRACE

Aye, I thought it might be. Nip out the back, Edie, and fetch me that box I told you about.

Exit EDIE. Enter WALKER.

WALKER

You all packed up, Grace? It's high time you were out of this place. Nowt but ghosts for you now, I guess.

GRACE

Well, there were good times, John, and there were other times, too. It was a good home to us, Bell House, but they're all gone now, – David, William, Isaac and all the rest – all gone.

WALKER

But Isaac has kept himself out of trouble these last years; living in White Lee, so I hear.

GRACE

He's gone. Gone from here, gone from Bell House, gone from my life.

WALKER

Now, you know what I've come about, lass?

GRACE

Oh, aye, you'll get the brass for the farm, all right.

Enter EDIE with a box, which she gives to GRACE, who passes it on to WALKER.

Here. Count it if you want.

WALKER empties gold coins from the box onto the table and counts them back into the box.

WALKER

All full weight, are they? Do I need my scales?

GRACE

Nay, lad. Nothing clipped here; they're all full weight. And anyway, you'll never see a clipped coin this side of Halifax again.

Exit WALKER.

Goodbye, Bell House, the court of King David. From here we ruled the world. The yellow trade was our salvation. For a while it was in our blood, but the world has moved on. They came from afar not to help us, only to crush us, because we dared to touch their gold. In the end, there is no gold but that in our hearts, no grace but what we are born with. Gold to gold, blood to blood, dust to dust.

GRACE takes a final look around and exits.

Curtain.

END

Historical note

The key events depicted in this play are based on historical documents pertaining to the murder of William Dighton and the arrest and prosecution of David Hartley and other members of the coiners' gang. In some minor details, however, I have deviated from the historical timeline for dramatic purposes. For example, I have brought forward the involvement of Lord Rockingham, who did not in fact visit Halifax until after Dighton's murder.

Details such as the initial lack of interest on the part of central government, Lord Weymouth's unsavoury reputation in office, the Gold State Carriage, etc., although they have close parallels in our own times, are historically accurate. Whereas Weymouth's letter in Act II Scene 3 is invented, the quotation in Act V Scene 5 is genuine. William Chamberlayne, Solicitor to the Royal Mint, also referred to in that scene, arrived in Halifax in December 1769.

It is a matter of record that Grace Hartley bore three children (David, Mary and Isaac) during the years covered in the play and that she passed away in 1802 aged 61, but other than that little is known about the life she led or how her marriage to David Hartley, eleven years her senior, came about. It has previously been speculated that David Hartley brought her to Bell House from the Midlands, but there is evidence that her maiden name was Sutcliffe, which is a local surname in the Calder Valley, so this dramatisation incorporates both possibilities. Sutcliffe is also the name of the landlord from whom William Hartley rented Bell House, a fact which gave rise to the notion of the arranged marriage, a practice which at the time was by no means limited to the middle and upper classes.

Some key relationships have been simplified. David and Isaac had a younger brother, William, who however appears to have had little involvement with the coining business, and Isaac's wife Bessy had four children of her own to care for during the period of this drama. William Hartley was widowed earlier than is implied in the play.

Historically, there was a further go-between, one Thomas Spencer, who facilitated the involvement of the murderers, but his role has been transferred to Thomas Clayton.

The subsequent exploits of Clayton and Spencer could fill a volume, as could the trial and execution of Normington and Thomas. Indeed, there are a vast number of colourful characters about whom more could be written, such as Barbara Broadbent, landlady of Barbary's, the coiners' tavern in Mytholmroyd.

Hartley was arrested, not at their local haunt, but at The Old Cock Inn in Halifax, still open to this day.

Although the timeline has been compressed slightly, it is historically accurate that more than twenty coiners detained in York were released in April 1770, whereas Hartley, Oldfield and Varley were sentenced to death, with Oldfield's death sentence subsequently being quashed. David Hartley and James Oldfield were hanged in York at 2:30 pm on 28 April 1770.

www.ingramcontent.com/pod-product-compliance
Lightning Source LLC
Chambersburg PA
CBHW052005090426
42741CB00008B/1565